# POET FLYER

## WWII Poetry & Photographs Based on Aerial Combat

E. John Knapp

| | | |
|---|---|---|
| Library of Congress Control Number: | | 2009914089 |
| ISBN: | Hardcover | 978-1-4500-0975-1 |
| | Softcover | 978-1-4500-0974-4 |
| | Ebook | 978-1-4500-0976-8 |



This book was printed in the United States of America.

**To order additional copies of this book, contact:**
Xlibris Corporation
1-888-795-4274
www.Xlibris.com
Orders@Xlibris.com
67968

A collection of memories as poems based on WWII aerial combat

experiences in the European Theatre of War

In the U.S. Army Air Corps

of the 100th Bomb Group Heavy

with the 349th bomb squadron of B17 "Flying Fortresses"

1942 to 1945, or thereabouts.

by 1st Lieutenant E. John Knapp, Navigator

dedicated

to

Maxine

my wife

my partner

my mentor

dedicated to the

nine young men

of my B-17 crew

who were lost

in combat in 1944

## INSPIRATION

THE INSPIRATION to write my
WWII combat flying experiences
into a POETRY book
came from my three wonderful children,
Marcia, Laura and Eric.
They urged me to write this book in POETRY.
During the last sixty-four years I rarely talked to them
about my war experiences. Many vets did the same.
The war was over and my life was now on the good side.
They wanted me to tell them my experiences in combat.
It only took me sixty years to tell them some of the
true stories of the courageous men I flew with.

—E. John Knapp

# POET FLYER

*WWII Poetry and Photographs Based on Aerial Combat*

*By E. John Knapp, 1st Lieutenant Navigator*
With assistance from Marcia Knapp Krech

## FORWARDS



# CONTENTS

# THE VOICE OF A POEM

A poem creeps
Softly
Into my thirsty thought
It starts a stir inside
My sometimes
Thinking

This poem's voice is
Not silent
Not fastened in phonics
Not loud as a howl shout
Not caught in rehearsed
Rhetoric

A poem has a
Gentle voice
When I listen softly for its
Voicing
It creeps but is not creepy
It stirs ideas but what's
Stirring
It runs but who's
Racing

A poem's voice rarely softly sits
And says just a little
Is this voice
Quieted
Or only just metered
When the poem is
Rhyming
I choose to listen
Carefully

Poetry talks to me
Every time
I chose to listen
And I seek the
Soft voice of a poem
Each time I'm carefully
Reading

# CHAPTER #1

# World War II Starts

# CADET STATUS
## Phase 1

I had enlisted
In the Army Air Corps
And was already singing
"You're in the Army now"
by April of 1941

Max and I ignored the advice of many
That in wartime
Marriage has survival problems
"The war is coming soon for our country."
They admonished us many times

I was 'he' alone
Max was 'she' alone
We became 'us' together
They were not 'us'
They did not know our hearts
So we married August of 1941
We established an especially good 'us' together

We felt war had descended directly upon 'us'
Starting in December 1941
The Air Corps called me up as a cadet
I left home in February 1942

We hugged a "so-long" on
The streets of downtown Detroit
With Mom and Dad too
We knew not even separation
Would end this good 'us' marriage

First a tough physical exam
They found live warm bodies
Second a long written exam
The Army found able minds
I passed with flying colors

We twenty-five new cadets
Rode the railroad passenger cars
A long time to Nashville Gulch
To an Air Corps induction center

The previous cadets welcomed us
They lined up along the roadway
As we marched to our first barracks

Yelling
"You'll be sorry" over and over again
Which had a confusing meaning to us

We found the food to be mediocre
We found the army cots hard
We found the barracks cold
You're in the army now

Which do you want
Pilot—copilot—navigator—bombardier
OK all will go to pilot pre flight school
So we all headed to pilot school

**John and Maxine Before the War.** Maxine is sitting on my lap in front of my parent's home. She had a smile on her face. We were a happy newlywed couple. I was concerned with the prospect of leaving architectural college and joining the Army Air Corps. How will my status as a newlywed be challenged? The news of the bombing of Pearl Harbor is just a few days away.

**The Student Architect.** In November of 1941, I was a newlywed and a sophomore studying architecture and engineering at Lawrence Tech University in Detroit, Michigan, working on the design and planning of a building project for my professor. I had plenty of math and engineering assignments to study for my evening classes. The news of the attack on Pearl Harbor had not hit me yet.

# CADET STATUS
## Phase 2

They eventually reassigned me
With many other cadets to
Navigation school in Monroe, Louisiana
It was like studying back in college
Learn and know—learn then fly—learn more navigation

Study-study every day and most nights
Practice celestial navigator flights
I flew and navigated every other night
Taking exams almost every day

One day I was looking down at my study desk
Studying navigator problem assignments
Out of the blue came a loud "Ten hut!"
And a gentle "At ease."

I looked up and saw a tall Captain
Standing by my classroom desk
Glory be! It was my longtime college buddy
Captain Ed
Glory be! Ed and I walked outside
And enjoyed a wonderful discussion

How glad I was to have a friend who
Has returned from aerial combat
In the south Pacific
He was my Air Cadet commanding officer
For the rest of my navigation studies here
My spirit and morale were lifted

**Flyer Knapp.** As an aviation cadet, I'm standing in front of my barracks waiting to fly a celestial navigation learning mission at night in southern Louisiana. My status as a newlywed has been changed from "us" to "he," many long miles apart from "she."

# CADET STATUS
## Phase 3

What happens when another cadet screws up in town?
What happens isn't nice
One unruly cadet
One fight with an MP and
That unruly cadet had a free ride back to base

With one angry Colonel's orders
The entire Cadet Corps
Was confined
To base for the weekend

I called my dear Maxine in town
Can't have a pass this weekend
She had just arrived in Monroe, Louisiana
All the cadet wives were upset
That weekend

Glory be! Captain Ed found out
All cadets were confined to the base
Courageous Captain Ed confronted our Colonel
With a heated discussion

When it ended Captain Ed had
Three cadet weekend passes
Signed by the Colonel
Three cadets and three wives were elated
Now the MPs at the gate had to let us out

Captain Ed owned a car and gas rations
Captain Ed had arranged a watermelon party
And hamburgers with onions
At a Monroe city park
For the three cadets and wives
My two friends and I had a great weekend

We wanted to pin a medal
On Captain Ed
We were headed overseas to a place
Where there were no watermelon picnics
In the European war
There would no be picnics either

We learned a lot of navigation
From Ed's true combat stories
We got him talking about his missions
At the watermelon party

We were
Spitting watermelon seeds
While the Germans were
Spitting bullets
All too soon we cadets would be Lieutenant navigators
Flying B-17s and
Spitting our own bombs
Back on the Nazi war machine

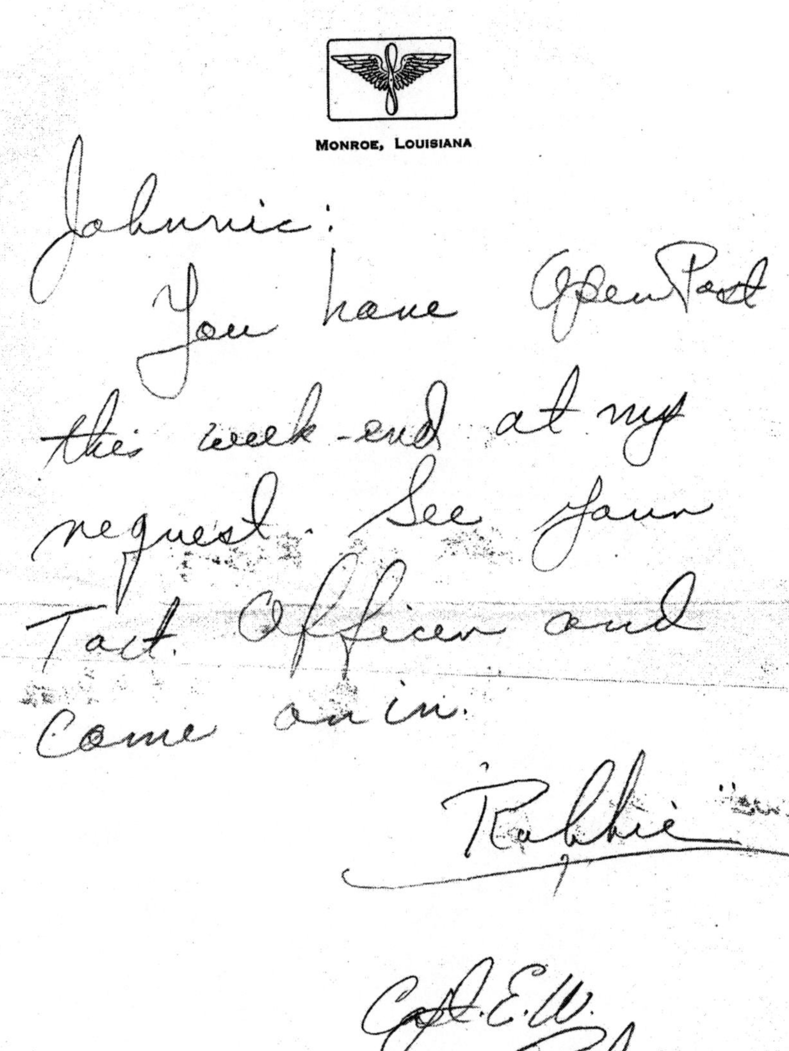

MONROE, LOUISIANA

Johnnie:

You have Open Post this week-end at my request. See your Tact. Officer and come on in.

Robbie

Capt. E. W. Robinson

**Captain Ed's Note.** This open-post note from Captain Ed Robinson allowed my two buddies and I to get off the base in Monroe, Louisiana to attend a watermelon party, during the summer of 1943. Captain Ed and I were good friends at Lawrence Tech in Detroit.

**Maxine and Captain Ed.** This beautiful photo is of my lovely wife Maxine next to our hero, Captain Ed Robinson. Two of my cadet friends and I and our wives attended Captain Ed's watermelon party.

**Picnic in the Trunk.** This interesting photo of Captain Ed's watermelon party is in Monroe, Louisiana. This party gave us aviation cadets some rest and lifted our morale. To associate with a real combat navigator was a learning opportunity.

# CHAPTER #2

# Combat Training

# WE MADE IT

They pulled an old train
Out of a railroad warehouse
Passenger cars were mostly wood
Somebody swept the floors
And brushed off the wooden seats

The Captain herded us new 2nd Lieutenants
Onto those old train cars
In Monroe, Louisiana for a long slow trip
To some place in Texas

After several hours of
Slow travel on a slow train
An Air Corps Captain showed up and informed us
We were headed for Pyote, Texas

Destination: Rattlesnake Bomber Base
Way down in southeastern Texas
Here we would be assigned to a crew
And introduced to a B-17 Flying Fortress

The conductor revealed he would
Let us off at Pyote, Texas
A GI truck would pick us up
And convoy us to the base

Twenty-five tired and hungry
Pilots and airmen stepped off
That old railroad train
And saw no city south of the tracks

As the old train pulled away
We saw not much more city
North of the tracks just desert sand
Where the blankety-blank
Did they dump us off to?

A good half an hour of sweating
And a GI truck finally showed up
All twenty-five men and their baggage
Climbed on for some destination
And here we come

This part of Texas was a dry desert
With a few scrawny trees
And many oil well towers
We couldn't see much else

Rattlesnake Bomber Base
Was a typically bleak Army Base
Would I see any rattlesnakes
Hiding in the surprising green grass?

The truck driver unloaded us
In front of a GI barracks
And said, "Here it is.
Welcome home!"

Another Captain showed up and
Read us our orders then
Marched us to the much needed mess hall
Food was welcome and quite good

Then we marched to the assembly hall
With about a hundred other officers

The Major welcomed us and
Started to call off names
He was assembling B-17 Flight Crews
Of four officers each
Pilot Copilot Navigator Bombardier

The Major called Jim McGuire, Pilot
Next he called Randy Bradley, Copilot
They would be two short pilots
Flying a big B-17 bomber
They shook hands for the first time

Next he called John Knapp, Navigator
I stood up and greeted the two pilots
Lastly he called John Jones, Bombardier
With greetings and handshakes
We four became a B-17 flight crew

Then six gunners were called up
And our gun crew was formed
We all wondered which one was to be
The lead engineer and top gunner
Sergeant Frank DeGeorge raised his hand
We were a complete crew

Now where was our B-17, Flying Fortress?

**The James McGuire Crew.** Our full crew in front of a B-17, Heavy Bomber. My crew had ten men, ten new friends. We had just formed a combat crew about to fly in our B-17 Flying Fortress to England.

Front Row L-R: Lt. James McGuire, Pilot; Randell Bradley, Co-Pilot; Lt. E. John Knapp, Navigator; Lt. John Jones, Bombardier.
Back Row L-R: Sgt. John Ribuffo, Ball Turret; Sgt. Frank DeGeorge, Engineer-Top Gunner; Sgt. Donald Kuntz, Gunner; Sgt. Rodney McCaughin, Radio Operator; Sgt. Alan Dill, Waist Gunner; Sgt. John Sabotka, Tail Gunner.

## DAMN FOOLISHNESS

I once had a friend who was a
Bombardier during World War II
In the US Army Air Corps
He was a bit of a hot head

He was good at his job
But a nonconformist
He was married
And could fly into a rage on a dime

My pilot Jim and wife Lou
Along with my wife Maxine and I
Lived for a few months
In a small house off base in Pyote, Texas

The small house had three bedrooms
We needed only two of them
So Hot Head and his wife
Moved into the third bedroom

Another friend was also a bombardier
Who unknown to us had very
Wandering eyes and
We soon found out how wandering

Wandering Eyes came to
Visit us one evening
Hot Head was flying that night and
His wife took a shine to Wandering Eyes

Hot Head came home early that night
And caught his wife making time with
Wandering Eyes and guess what
We heard a lot of noise

The front door slammed shut
Wandering Eyes had left fast
But the arguing noise went on
Hot Head was beating his wife

Pilot Jim and I stopped him
But the arguing noise went on
Hot Head left the house angry and upset
We went back to sleep

Is this the end of the story?
Oh no!
Not by any means in this war
Once we all got to England

Both bombardiers
Flew combat missions in occupied Europe
Both bombardiers
Were shot down over enemy territory

Both were captured and thrown into a Nazi POW camp
Hot Head had a small bed in the prison camp
And guess who was assigned next to him
Wandering Eyes!

The fortunes of war are never logical
These two bombardiers grew up fast
They learned they were not enemies
They combined forces to survive POW life

Having lived through the experience of
Being shot down . . . parachuting from sky
Into enemy hands
Changes a man forever

They found inner qualities they
Didn't know were in them
After being in enemy hands
Seeing your fellow prisoners as buddies

Today I wonder
Did what they learned in prison camp
Come home with them
Did they remember what they had become

As a citizen veteran
Back in civilian life
Did they remember they were different?
Did they ever see each other again?

# JIM OUR PILOT

Jim was what we called him
But his full name was
Lieutenant James W. McGuire, Pilot

We immediately accepted Jim McGuire
As our Pilot Commander
We became a working flight crew
Under Jim's leadership

Jim was a small man
5′ 4″ and 140 pounds
His co-pilot Brad was small, too
5′ 5″ and 145 pounds
Jim was a smart leader
With a good flight record

We had great fun watching these
Two small pilots on the controls
Landing this big four-engine B-17 Bomber
Named by Jim "The Denver Doll"
After his wife Lou

Jim arranged for the B-17 crew photo
He found a home for the wives
In the little town of Pyote, Texas
So the officers could stay in town with their wives

Jim had a good wife
He revered her and sought her advice
Jim had a daughter, Jane
The apple of his eye
He was a family man

There were ten men on the crew
Of our B-17 airplane
Our success was working together as
One
Commander Jim understood this
He became our leader quickly
Not just our boss

**Jim and Lou McGuire.** My Pilot Jim McGuire and his wife Lou in 1942 in Denver right before Jim left for pilot training in the U.S. Army Air Corps.

**Jim and his daughter Jane.** Pilot Jim and his daughter while he was in training in Pyote, Texas, at Rattlesnake Bomber base. This pretty little daughter was the apple of Jim's eye. He was a devoted father. Jim and his crew left for England soon after this photo was taken. The house in the background is mentioned in the poem, DAMN FOOLISHNESS.

**John and Jim.** Navigator Lieutenant John Knapp and Pilot Lieutenant Jim McGuire on the front porch of their rented house in Pyote, Texas. They are the leaders of the flying team soon headed for the ETO.

# WING IT

We wondered what would happen
at our newly assigned Nebraska Army air base
We wondered where
in the world was our destination
We were full of anticipation
of the battle to come
Were ready now to encounter WWII

A goodbye was squeezed out
to our wives and family
Late one night

Our big bird's four engines
were roaring to go
with ten flyers a ready team.
The big bird would take off and
Head east a thousand miles and greater
Eastern Canada, the first stop

But we had an important detour
The wives were quartered a couple miles
Off the runway
They had enjoyed our last kiss and smile

But now we would bestow
a last goodbye signal
We buzzed over their hotel, low
Wagged our wings up and down
As they waved back

Over their hotel
Over the air base
Over the USA
Over the Atlantic

The stars above looked good along our course
        Guiding our flight
The moon above smiled
        Divulging our flight direction

So did the low clouds
        For England's clouds were our goal

**B-17 Flying Fortress.** A peacetime B-17 Flying Fortress parked in the Jefferson City, Missouri airport in 2006. Many veterans and civilians came to see this beautiful old fighting airplane. Many crawled inside and saw the cramped spaces. Not much space but we all did our job without complaining.

# CHAPTER #3

# Combat Missions

# AND HERE WE ARE

We were flyers but they delivered us
By GI bus
A truck with a canvas top
Long wooden benches on each side
All our luggage piled up in the center
And here we are arriving

It was a late afternoon in February
We were tired and hungry
Glad the long flight trip was over
From Nebraska, U.S.A. to Thorpe Abbotts, England
The prefab concrete Officers' barracks
Looked good
And here we are arriving

There were ten of us
A full B-17 crew assigned
To the 100$^{th}$ Bomb Group
We were trained and experienced
In B-17 flying but considered rookies
But here we are anyway

We four Officers unloaded and
Our six-man gunner crew was
Driven on to their barracks
We walked inside

The first four beds were vacant—assigned to us
Four Officers had moved their beds
Towards the rear of the barracks
And here we are now

The barracks held sixteen men
For four combat crews' Officers
The three other crews welcomed us warmly
And here we are as replacements

We exchanged Air Corps niceties
Discovered Pilot Jim from Denver
Co-pilot Brad from Texas
Navigator John from Detroit
Bombardier John from Mississippi
And here we are from all over

Each of us picked out one of
The four vacant crew beds
And started unpacking
A GI bus arrived
To deliver us to Headquarters
For briefing and orientation

Six rookie crews equal to sixty men
Had been lost in aerial combat
So far this year
And here we are
A Rookie crew just arrived
Replacing one of those crews

No one told us we were assigned to the
Eighth Air Corps, called
The Bloody Hundredth Group
"Famous" for losing so many courageous flyers

After a day of practice formation flying
A good night's sleep and several GI meals
We were ready for our first combat mission
Over Nazi-occupied Europe
Rousted up early before sunrise
And I thought, "We really are here."

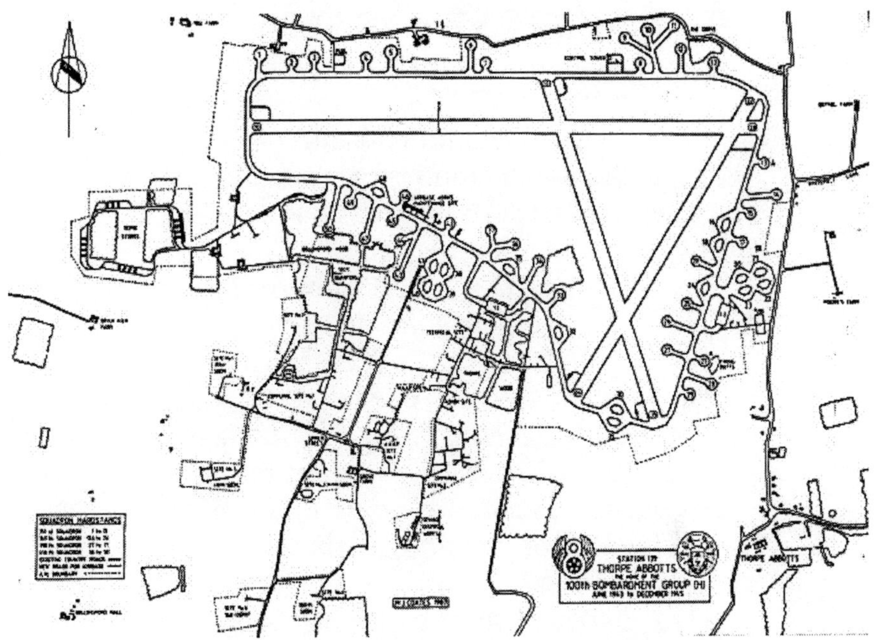


**Map of Thorpe Abbots in 1944.** The 100th Bomb Group base in Thorpe Abbotts, England was built by the Royal Air Force. When the forward squadron of the U.S. Air Force arrived, they found a complete facility for the Group. It had been an active Royal Air Force flyer base. The forward squad was able to inform the four Air Corps bomb squadrons and all support facilities they could come to Thorpe Abbotts as the 100th Bomb Group in England.

## MY FIRST MISSIONS

Rookie crew or no
We got the same treatment as the veterans
Always Standard Operating Procedure
We learned quickly
For this was the first mission for
The McGuire crew

We were rousted out of bed at 4:00 a.m.
Quick dressing . . . quick breakfast
Very thorough mission target briefing
A Nazi airport we never heard of
I checked all my equipment six times

My E-6-B navigator's graphic calculator
Was a handy slide rule
Helped me figure out ground speed and directions
Necessary and non-electronic

Weather briefing was not favorable
Cloudy on takeoff and cloudy over target
Typical lousy Europe flying
Our Group took off anyway
Fifteen big B-17s one at a time
I was thankful for my G-box
Code for "Radar navigation"

About a dozen fighter planes escorted us
From English coast to European coast
Then returned to England, low on gas
I watched German ME-109s pick us up
No room for fear
I navigated us toward our target

The Nazi defense
Lined the Europe coastline
With flack guns almost continuously but
They left a few holes to control our routes
Ready to ambush our bombers as we snuck in

Their crude radar couldn't follow
All our routes to our targets
So their ambush plans sometimes failed

As soon as we penetrated the coastline
Heavy clouds covered our route for miles ahead
Bombers in formation can't fly through clouds
So after ten minutes of flight
The Lead Pilot radioed, "Abandon mission."
We made a long 180° turn back to home base

So this was our first combat mission
Our first view of 100th BG from the air and landing
We were no longer rookies
But we weren't seasoned flyers yet
What was to come?
Who knew?

Crews were required to be de-briefed
By S-2 Intelligence staff
What did we observe—even on short or aborted missions?
Did we see any enemy activity
Did we see any coastal construction

Lunch and sack time next
Even an aborted mission lasted four hours
What was in store for us tomorrow
I went to sleep wondering

In our first month we flew many missions
One crew completed their tour and returned home
We lost a couple of planes and crews
Our barracks lost one
Crew of four men so

We moved our crew beds
Towards the rear of the barracks
Making the first four beds vacant for
The next replacement
Rookie crew

**Formation Flying**. Contrails of a B-17 group in formation flying at high altitude, perhaps 35,000 feet. When gasoline burns in an engine it exhausts mostly water vapor and carbon dioxide, which freezes and forms white contrails at this altitude.

# RIVETS

They made our big bird
        with rivets
They cut aluminum sheets
fastening one curved sheet to another
        with rivets in lines
Every few feet added rounded aluminum ribs
        with rivets around and around inside
bracing the skin to bird shape

Radio guy's crew desk
        is riveted
holding his radios
His floor is sheeted and
        riveted strong

Navigator's desk is a firmed sheet
        braced and riveted
to rounded ribs
holding his maps
Floor is sheeted and
        riveted strong

After many buckets of rivets
We see this big aluminum bird
        perched on the ground
        and the rivets
        and the skin
        and the ribs
        and the riveted tail
        and the riveted wings
all together can fly . . . up high . . . in the sky

Who's too nervous to fly
so high in the sky
saying "bye-bye"
to enemy targets
        way down below

No. I'm not nervous. I'm just scared.
Flying straight and level
toward this day's target 30,000 feet
        way down below

As those puffs of black flack smoke
        move closer
        and closer

Some counted us courageous
Some counted us heroes
But I counted rivets around and around
finally reached 1,999
And yelled, "When in sam hill
        will our load drop?"

Our big bird jumped up higher
as our giant bomb load
        dropped away.
Our big bucket of rivets
        shook with relief
        as our load was delivered
completing our job for Uncle Sam

We "Heiled" our enemy
        dumping our big load
on his ailing war machine
        way down below

Now
Our flight crew worked for us and flew
        our big bucket of rivets
        our big bird
        our squadron of big birds
        our escort fighter birds
All heading back
toward our English home base.

It took a huge effort by us all to bring war's end closer.
        Even all the rivets
This day's assignment was accomplished
Scared alive alert grateful
Onward we went to another day

My squadron was not hurt that day
My crew was alive that day
I felt relief for being alive that day

**Bomb Bay.** The interior of a B-17 bomb bay seen in a B-17 in Jefferson City, Missouri. I count fourteen "bombs" in the racks. This would have been a typical bomber load for any mission flying over Nazi-occupied Europe in 1943.

# KNOCKED OUT OF FORMATION

Our fourth mission
No longer rookies
Flying over big Nazi industry
Bombardier dropped our bomb load
Huge Nazi railroad yard was hit

Top gunner hollered
Bogies twelve o'clock high
A whole squad of Nazi fighters ME-109s
Gunners started shooting

Our tight bomber formation
Concentrated gunner fire power
Best protection for the group
A lone bomber is easy Nazi fighter prey

Our lead Major . . . a Rookie
Panicked and broke formation
Heading his plane home
Our number three engine was hit
We were knocked out of formation

Our whole bomber squadron broke formation
And scattered
"Navigator to Pilot! Hit those clouds!"
German fighters hate clouds and won't come in after us
We were flying blind
But I knew the route home

We flew blind in the clouds for fifteen minutes
No fighters no friendly squadron
Then the clouds opened up a little
Wow . . . down below I saw the city of
Quekenbruck, Germany

This City had been yesterday's target
I knew the return route to our home base
Three good engines will fly us okay
Our plane limped across the Channel
Headed for the Thorpe Abbots runway

One engine out caused a hard left drift
We just missed the control tower
Our landing was bumpy but
We landed . . . crew safe and intact
England never looked so good
Dinner sure tasted downtown

Most of the squadron returned
Without following us into the clouds
I never knew how they got home
Only three planes didn't return

We knew the rookie Major
Would be in trouble
The General's critique mission meeting
Early next morning was loud and tough
The Major was on a plane back
To the U.S.A.
The following morning

What's up for tomorrow's mission?

**Planes Heading Toward Clouds.** Navigator to Pilot, "Hit those clouds! Nazi fighters won't follow!"

# THE BIG 'B' MISSION

Over Berlin, Germany
Our radio crewman screamed
On the intercom
"Pilot! Pilot!
Bomb bay's full of smoke!"

Pilot Jim immediately lowered
The plane's wheels
As a signal of distress
To our flight squadron formation

Jim grabbed the bomb salvo lever
Released the entire bomb load
But kept our plane in
Squadron formation

Getting rid of our smoking bomb load
Was typical of Jim's cool command
Our crew knew he would do the right thing
At the right time

The target of the day was
The big railroad station in Berlin
Nazis used this station to dispatch
Infantry troops to fight Allies

The squadron's bombs hit
The railroad station and
Our salvoed bombs hit
The railroad tracks

Next the bombardier, John Jones
Went back into bomb bay
Hand cranked the bomb bay doors shut
He found the door's motor
Had burned out
Wow . . . that was a close call

Our flight back to home base
In England was routine
No opposition
We all landed safe and sound

**Strike Photo of Berlin Railroad Yard.** The Group's bomb strike hit the target. The McGuire plane dumped its bombs on the railroad yard as a salvoed bomb strike. This strike photo shows that the bomb loads of the squadron hit the Berlin railroad yards.

# RESCUE

It was a cold and wet morning
It would heat up soon
The Sergeant woke us up at 4:30 a.m.

A special mission today, Lieutenant
There is a B-17 crew down
In the North Sea
And the water is very cold

Your B-17 crew is assigned to
Search, find and rescue this downed crew

You will carry a rubber boat
No bombs . . . only 50-caliber machine guns

We flew a search and rescue pattern over the water
I gave the pilot two headings
North 5° and South 185°

First we flew North at a 5° heading
For 30 minutes
Then a slow left U-turn South at a 185° heading
For 30 minutes

Then a slow right U-turn North at a 5° heading
For 30 minutes which was 75 miles
I adjusted for wind change each half hour
We searched over 300 square miles on each heading
In two hours we searched over 1600 square miles

I asked Pilot Jim to descend to 1000 feet
So we could see the downed plane or raft better
And be under enemy radar
We never saw a Jerry fighter

We had sunshine all morning
I called on our plane's intercom to the crew
Find our airplane's shadow on water below
The downed crew will appear
Smaller than our water shadow

After searching for hours
Headquarters ordered us home

We looked and looked but never found
That downed B-17 crew on the sea
I tried to find out what happened
I'm still waiting and wondering

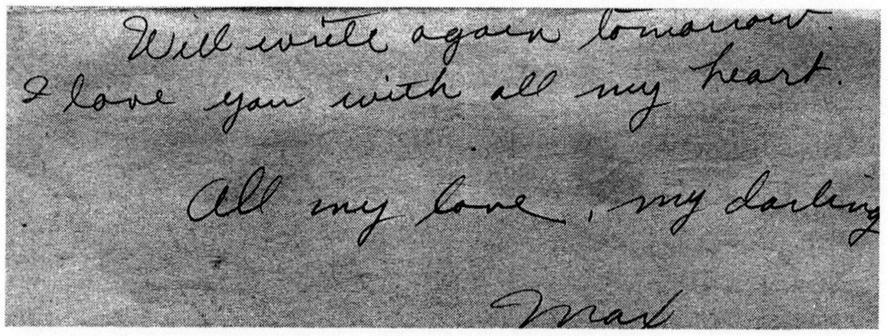

Will write again tomorrow.
I love you with all my heart.

All my love, my darling

Max

**A Typical Maxine Letter.** I loved getting letters from Maxine. A fellow couldn't ask for a more supportive wife.

# WAITING

6th Mission

I'm waiting and wondering
And still a waiting Navigator
        Where *are* they?
In the sky, flying high?
Or on the ground?
        Where *are* they bound?

My ten-man crew,
Without its Navigator,
        (I was abruptly pulled off by the Colonel)
My group took off with eleven other
Heavy Bombers, in V-formation
Carrying tons of bombs
        Destination:
        Nazi secret weapons site

A short mission without its Navigator
        Target on the French coast
Now I am waiting for my crew's return
Where *are* they?
Are they late?
        Or
something else?

I stood at the runway's end
Counting and counting
        and still counting
Numbers one through ten
        landed
Waiting and waiting
        Still waiting for eleventh and twelfth
        to land

Here comes our Sergeant in a jeep
"Sorry, Lieutenant,
Your crew went down, direct flak hit
over Cherbourg, France."

Much silence
and too much waiting
can't hold back tears
"Any parachutes?"
"Yeah, three."

My waiting appeared over
My worry was answered
My concern had been too real

When a navigator cries
over the loss of nine friends
nine buddies
What can he say?
What can he do?
What did he say?

I could call them brave
I could call them courageous
But I must call them . . . gone

Why am I alone? . . .
Why am I still wondering? . . .

. . . and still waiting . . . ?

**B-17s Pealing Off at Thorpe Abbotts.** A squadron of B-17s approaching the runway as they peel off from their V-formation and land at their 100th BG home base. A squadron of B-17s forms a long line of planes landing on the up-wind runway.

**B-17s Landing at Thorpe Abbotts.** This maneuver allowed all the planes to land one at a time with an easy landing distance. They make a beautiful group of planes flying in the sky after returning from a combat mission.

## AND HERE I AM

In my second month my crew
Without their navigator
Was shot down over Cherbourg
Leaving my three crew beds vacant

That night I tried sleeping next to those
Three vacant crew beds
With prayer and fatigue I drifted
Into troubled sleep

The next day I moved to an empty bed
At the rear of the barracks
As was the custom here
Making the first four vacant crew beds
Waiting for a replacement
Rookie crew

And here they will be
When they show up
The four beds await them

The next day I was not rousted out of bed
Early before daylight
A stand down . . . I slept till 7:00 a.m.
I decided to take for a bath
Then I shaved and had breakfast

It looked like a good day to visit the
Combat crew library
Amazing what I learned
The experienced pilots and navigators
Reported on the rough missions they flew

The written accounts and facts
Of their missions were tacked
On the wall of the library along with
Photos of bomb strikes on targets
Damage assessments by S-2

I poured over those combat reports
By many B-17 crews
About the missions they flew
I studied the strike photos
Of a recent mission I had flown
And how we had hit our assigned target
I had discovered S-2 was
The single source of recorded combat knowledge

I came away wanting to talk with
The S-2 officers for they
Kept the records of combat missions
And were the source for
Secret combat information

**War Buddies.** Here I am with some of the friends I made after I lost my crew. They meant a lot to me because I was never assigned to a permanent crew again. I was an extra navigator assigned to where ever I was needed. World War II made flying buddies into longtime friends as you can see in this photo of navigators and bombardiers. Background shows trees of the woods surrounding the bomber base. Left rear: John, then Paul, third unknown, kneeling is George Morgan.

# COOK'S MEDAL

The 100th Bomb Group had a good cook
He had a good smile
He made GI meals into tasty dinners
Using the food he had to work with

Flyers had a special mess hall #1
All 300 Enlisted flyers ate in mess hall #2
The Officers' Club had their mess hall #3

One day the Officers asked the cook for
Boston baked beans
He said he had been waiting for this request
The baked beans were wonderful
He served them in the Officers' mess hall #3
There were no beans left over

The flyers could not be served beans
In mess hall #1 anyway
Because beans caused cramps at high altitude

One day when the flyers returned from their mission
Needing sack time and chow
Cookie made some delish hot cross buns
For the returning crews of both men and officers

What a delight!
What a morale builder!
What a welcome for returning flyers!
The GI gunners said Cookie should get a medal

The Major agreed
So he wrote up a recommendation
In his flowery official language and
Sent it to the Colonel

The Colonel signed the letter
And sent it to the General
The General sent back the Bronze Star
And the Major pinned the Star
On our hero the Sergeant Cook
Ain't the Army Air Corps grand!

**Nighttime Routine.** George Morgan, a bombardier friend and I are about to brush our teeth. With our pajamas on, we will hit the sack soon. Neither of us knows where tomorrow's combat mission will take us.

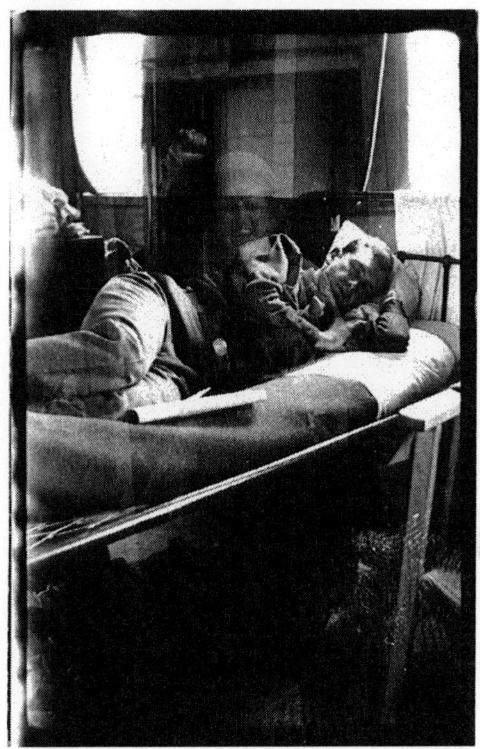

**Sack Time.** Getting some extra sleep was important and priceless to us flyers in the Thorpe Abbotts barracks. Here I'm catching some sack time after a long flight. Notice the double-exposed smiling GI face. I never knew who he was or how that happened.

# A HIT

(One early summer morning at
100th Bomb Group Air Base)

During a combat mission briefing
Whoopp . . . Whamm . . . Blamm
Run scamper race
Here we go
To air raid shelters

What happened
What was that loud noise
Gunners said single German fighter
Dumped a couple of small bombs
On our runway
Small bombs . . . big noise . . . small craters
Brazen nuisance

Group briefing had a short delay
For today's mission
We needed a quick response

Trucks are coming
Repair of small craters are fixed quick
Two trucks of gravel
One truck of blacktop
Several hard-working men
Delay less than one hour

Now runway is fixed and ready
For takeoffs
Back to briefing flyers go

We will hit a German fighter airport
With a dozen B-17s
Each dropping
Twelve 500-pound bombs

Our 144-bombs answer

# MIND'S PUZZLED FLIGHT

**or the Adoration of a Woman**

Written by 1st Lieutenant E. John Knapp in 1944
While stationed at the 100th Bomb Group Base, Thorpe Abbotts, England

Now every day in some small way,
I try to make a scene
That brings up to my lonesome brain,

A picture of Maxine,
A picture, yes,
Or perhaps something
That we will do some day.
Or perhaps we won't feel like it
But only lounge around and say.

Now every time in my own way,
I try to make this scene,
The dimensions of my mind are easily pulled down,
And anything of importance
Is thrown across the scene.
I see a little ray of light
That falls about the day.
It jumps about all my thoughts and never seems to stay.
To stay, but why?
and then I have the fight.

To try to put the strange thing out,
And keep some thoughts
that are envisioned right.
But who the devil says?
Not that every time I think,
Not that every brain thought,
Rids a poet's pragmatic ray of light.
But that every scene that my tired and lonesome
Brain comes upon, has that little dancing ray
of light, that I have so often tried
To capture and name.

To capture and name!
    Perhaps,
    Yes, perhaps this is the little scene
    That I have tried to make.
Perhaps this the every day that
    Dances about my brain.
That leaps from moment to moment,
    And I never seem to gain.
But can tell some day there'll come
    A time, when all my imagination might,
    That I encompass, in my tired and lonesome
    Brain will set itself along a
Straightened line, and stay in just one place,
    Just long enough for that little dancing ray of light
    To dance along,
    To dance along and touch each little
Brain wave with its starry flash of light.

To have my tired and lonesome brain become,
    Wed to all this light,
    This little dancing ray of light.
That when each day in some small way,
I try to see that scene, Yes
    the one of Maxine.
    Don't forget now
    To have that little dancing ray of light
Dance along the line and touch each
Bit of lonesome brain wave and
Change it all.
    No! Not really change,
    But give it all "Imagination Might."
"Imagination Might" is what I really need.

Now every day I take my way
And try to think something new,
        To think of some small pay
        To have the little dancing ray of light
To dance along the line in one set place.
And give to my imagination
        "Imagination Might."

Now how can that be?
Sounds rather of an affirmative ordeal,
When the mind of man
        and the mind of an unknown
        Are to wed!
So let's all try and then we may know
        To get a sly system or a sly trick
        That won't let it go.
The dancing ray of light you know, I mean.

Now came a day in my own way,
        I was trying to make the scene,
The scene where in my tired and lonesome brain,
        I hook up imagination's screen,
        And try to make the picture
Of my own, my dear Maxine.
When flash across my picture's face,
        Came the little dancing ray of light,
When came to my tired and lonesome brain
        A system that seemed right.

Of how with clever handling,
I'd capture now the little dancing ray of
        Light, and have it touch
        Each bit of brain wave,
        And make
        But let's go on How to do?

Now here is the big idea:
Lets make a curving line that winding
        In and out,
        That winds around and around,
        And never stops,
        Let's play it way out.

Now if all the imagination might that I
Encompass in my own tired and lonesome brain,
        Shall set itself along this winding
        Curving line,
Not set in any one place,

Now every way each day it does,
        With all its dancing might,
        Bouncing back and forth,
Impelling into my tired and lonesome brain,
        The thing I have always wanted,
And the little dancing ray of light has
        Seemed to have flaunted,
        To put into, as it touched
My tired and lonesome brain,
        With
        "Imagination Might."

Now every day in my strong way
        As I do make the scene
        I see the little dancing ray of light,
        That always seems to stay,
        For I have found

That my imagination was really right.
        Yes, really right!
        For all the power that it did want,
        Was just a little "Imagination Might"

**Maxine before John Left.** My beautiful wife took a wonderful photo. Every time I looked at her photo overseas my eyes welled up and my tears flowed. Maxine had a soul that was as beautiful as her photo. Thank God the war ended and I got to go home to her as "us."

**John Before He Left**. After more than a year's Air Corps training I knew my crew and I were ready to fly overseas. No one looks forward to aerial combat. However we understood the Air Corps would bring the war to the Nazi homeland before the expected invasion. I had this portrait made for my wife Max before I left.

**Mind's Puzzled Flight.** Mixed Media by Anne Farley Gaines. Artwork I commissioned in the 1990's to accompany my poem written during the war. About a year into the war, my poetic genes started to run at high speed. This long poem began to form in my mind. I called this poem "The Adoration of a Woman" and named it "Mind's Puzzled Flight" because it was very difficult to be so far away from my lovely wife Maxine for so long. Read this poem and grasp the emotions many flyers felt for their families the same as I did. I think artist Anne Farley Gaines captured these feelings perfectly!

## OUR MOON

I used to fly up high in the sky
I flew the big ones
        up in Europe's high sky

And often above us
        was our moon
        glowing bright above us

Navigators have used
        our glowing moon for centuries,
        to find themselves on the sea
        at the north pole, exploring the earth
And up in the air, flying high

But I found a
        higher use, a private use,
For our moon, glowing brightly above us

I was in Europe in the sky
        flying up high
My wife was in the States in the mountains of Colorado
        looking up high into the sky

I wrote her the time
I would be up high in the sky
        seeing our moon's brightness

She wrote me the time
        she would be up high in the mountains
        seeing our moon's brightness

And there we were
        separated
        by ten thousand miles on Earth
But up high in the
        brightness of our moon
        we were together

My lonesome brain was calmed a little
I could fly and look up high in the sky
at the brightness of the moon
        For now it was OUR MOON

Wish very much that you could see the
beautiful moonlight nights that we are
having now. At 1900 in the evening (7 oc)
a big yellow moon pokes its head above
the edge of the world & smiles
at all of us over here. He looks
us all over & smiles as if to say
you should have seen what I just
left over in the U.S.A. He laughs at
us and makes us wish we could
blast him out of the sky. All the
time I have my mind on a beautiful
autumn night in the country side of
home. Take a long and deep look for
me Dear. Think of me as hard as
you can & perhaps I will catch a
bit of the beauty that only an
fall day or night is capable
of in the U.S.A.

**My Moon Letter to Maxine.** Here is part of the letter I refer to in OUR MOON.

Text: Wish very much that you could see the beautiful moonlight [moonlit] nights that we are having now. At 1900 in the evening (7:00) a big yellow moon pokes its head above the edge of the world & smiles at all of us over here. He looks us all over & smiles as if to say you should have seen what I just left over in the U.S.A. He laughs at us and makes us wish we could blast him out of the sky. All the time I have my mind on a beautiful autumn night in the country side of home. Take a long and deep look for me, Dear. Think of me as hard as you can & perhaps I will catch a bit of the beauty only a fall day or night is capable of in the U.S.A.

## WALKING BY GERMAN POWS

Captured German soldiers
Prisoners of war
Labored in the English potato fields
Near Thorpe Abbotts, England
Population fifty people

100$^{th}$ Bomb Group Air Corps Base
American Combat Group flying B-17s
Were living down the lane
Population five thousand men

Who does our laundry
I had soap and dirty clothes
Thorpe Abbotts had farmers
Living down the lane

We hired a Thorpe Abbots farmer's wife
To wash our socks
Paid her well

One day I was walking
Down the lane
And saw a dozen German POWs
Working in the English potato fields
With pitchforks, rakes and shovels

I was an American Lieutenant
In uniform
But I was hesitant
Being so near the enemy
With no gun

An English armed guard saw me
He knew my hesitation
"Hello, Yank!
I'll walk ye along."

So my laundry was done
Courtesy of a Thorpe Abbotts farmer's wife
And my fears were calmed
Courtesy of a British Army guard

**The Formans.** Mr. and Mrs. Forman, the English farmers of Thorpe Abbotts, Norfolk, UK. These fine people treated my crew just wonderful. They agreed to do our laundry and we provided the dirty clothing and the soap. They introduced us to English muffins and jam.

tonight we are
going out. that is we are going to go over to
our laundry lady's house for tea. You see
its so difficult to get laundry done that
we bribe them with stuff we get. We
found a half pound tea and with that she
took the laundry of all 4 men. We walk
in there and you just don't leave without
having tea & cakes. So we load up with
soap matches stuff and its a sure thing that
she will take all we bring. And on top of this
we sort of enjoy the business of going over to
an English home. She is sure glad to see us, and
we really don't bribe them. You understand only that
a little of some of the rational articles are appricated
so much.

**John's Letter to Max about the Formans.** In this letter I am telling Maxine all about the wonderful Mrs. Forman.

Text of Letter: Tonight we are going out, that is we are going out to our laundry lady's house for tea. It's so difficult to get laundry done that we bribe them with stuff we get. We found a half-pound tea and with that she took the laundry of all four men. We walk in there and you just don't leave without having tea and cakes. So we load up with soap, matches, stuff and it's a sure thing that she will take all we bring. And on top of this we sort of enjoy the business of going over to an English house. She's sure glad to see us and we really don't bribe them, you understand, only that a little of some of the rationed articles are appreciated so much.

# ALBERT HALL SYMPHONY, LONDON

Know what a Buzz Bomb was?
The Germans knew
The Londoners knew
The Americans knew

The first unmanned Nazi airplane
Carried a 500 pound bomb
With a noisy putt-putt engine
And enough fuel to reach London

Target: London . . . anyplace
They made a very loud put-put noise
Only 1500 feet altitude at 100 mph
When the engine stopped
The noise stopped
And the Buzz Bomb glided into the city
And exploded anyplace

Brits and Yanks were in Albert Hall one evening
Listening to the symphony
Roll of drums
The drummers lifted their drumsticks
The roll of the drums continued

A buzz bomb was overhead
The noisy putt-putt engine stopped
The Brits and Yanks knew
The target was nearby

The white stage lights turned into
Red air raid lights
The audience was quiet
The symphony continued playing
No one moved
We heard a big explosion
It missed the Hall

I admired the Brits that night
The Buzz Bomb did not move them
A little old grey haired lady said to me,
"Give up our culture for the Hun?
Never!"

**Buzz Bomb.** An aerial photo of a German pilotless buzz bomb headed for London. The pilot of the Spitfire fighter plane who took the photo soon shot this buzzer down. This one never reached London.

# D–DAY

The Free World was restless in 1944
They were calling:
Open up that second front!
Liberate occupied Europe from
The oppressive Nazi!

When it would happen
No one had knowledge
All understood secrecy was crucial
All waited impatiently
Both civilians and soldiers

At 4:00 a.m. before breakfast
The staff sergeant came and announced
Orders from the Colonel
Report to S2 Air Intelligence briefing room
**Now**

We were used to this type of order
And responded in the usual hurry
The flight crew navigators
Rushed to obey
The MP at the door said
**Show identification**
The first hint of a special mission
We'd never had to show ID before

The S2 briefing room had a huge
Wall map of all Europe
White stick pins indicated our
Many targets for the day
Red strings traced our flight routes
All routes and pins were to
French Normandy beach

The Colonel's command was
**You will not leave this briefing room**
Until flight time
You are here for an important mission today
Briefing is for D-Day
The invasion on French Normandy beaches
This is an absolute secret!

On this wall map note your targets
Here are maps and photos of the area
Study and learn target locations
Be sure you know how to find your target
You are helping the ground forces

We expect great resistance
From the enemy
Be alert
They will put up a lot of fighters
Enemy flak gunners will all be firing

Be alert
Tell your crew about the invasion
Only after your takeoff
The gunners need to know
But secrecy is crucial

Our Squadron put up 15 B-17s
A full flight effort
Our other three squadrons did the same
The 100th Group maximum effort was sixty B-17s
The 8th Army Air Corps flew over two thousand bombers
We began to understand this was
The big effort of WWII

All our targets were
Just ahead of the infantry and tanks
Off the Normandy beach
Great bombing precision was our mandate

At 12,000 feet we looked down
Saw thousands of boats filling the ocean below
We had to open our bomb bays
While over the water
And over the fleet
and over the men
I was terrified of a goof in bombing

Our target was right ahead in full sight
No Luftwaffe resistance yet
Very few flack bursts around us
Where were the Germans?
Our bombardier aimed carefully
His bombsight kicked out the bomb load
In a train of bombs fifty feet apart
Directly on target

These bombs awakened the Nazis ground troops
Or eliminated them
I patted our bombardier on the back
Good hit!

The six gunners on our B-17 never fired a shot
Our wings had no holes
The big resistance was zilch
We headed back to our home base
In Thorpe Abbots, England
Our Squadron had accomplished our task

I gave the pilot a northern compass heading
We began to see the squadron's landing strip
At our home base
We cheered on our good landing

Now we could finally get some breakfast
We walked silently into the mess hall
Our late breakfast was barely enjoyed

I looked around the mess hall
All the flight crews were wondering
If our bombing had helped the ground forces
And how were the infantry landings doing

The staff sergeant appeared
Get ready for the second mission today

**Strike Photo of our D-Day Mission.** This strike photo shows that we hit our invasion target on D-Day. My worry of a bombing goof was unfounded. Our target was a large Nazi gun emplacement that we silenced.

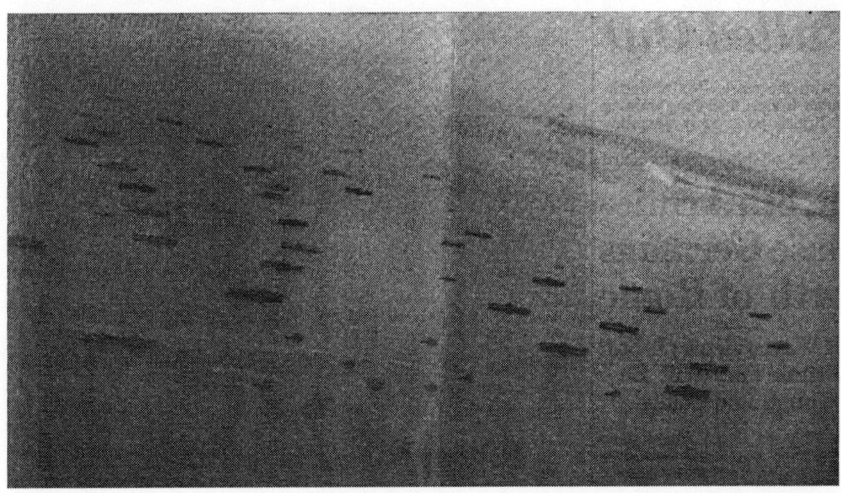

**Invasion ships from Stars and Stripes Newspaper.** The Stars and Stripes newspaper was published during WWII for all service people. I saved this newspaper photo of the hundreds of invasion ships approaching Cherbourg, France and landing on D-Day. This paper is sixty-five years old and hard to read. Look closely and see the many ships in this huge armada.

# D-DAY AFTERNOON

The Nazis had not quite understood
This was the real D-Day invasion
Their big armies were not in place yet
Behind the invasion beaches

After lunch our Colonel orders
Flight crews back into the big S2 briefing room
We must fly back to Normandy
Knock out the railroads and truck highways
A few miles behind the invasion beaches
Now is our chance to stop Nazi reinforcements

Briefing room is excited
Understanding this important mission
The big secret is out
We are all ready
We know our bombs will help

As soon as navigators and bombardiers
Study the maps and photos of
The railroads and highway targets
The crews were trucked out to their
B-17 Flying Fortresses—ready to go

Our squadron's fifteen aircraft lines up to take off
One plane accelerates down the runway
Every thirty seconds a bomber takes off
We fly around the radio beacon getting into our
Squadron's V-formation of a lead plane with two wing planes
In formation with stacked tiers of three B-17s

And here comes our squadron to help
Support the ground forces
Our many bombs act as
Their long-range artillery

I give our pilot a southern heading
We fly over the Channel
We see Normandy beach ahead
We look down on many ships
We see action fires explosions
Troops still landing

Our bomb bays open as we fly
Over Normandy's first couple of miles

Above the landings of men and tanks
I see railroad track targets
We fly straight and level with no evasive action
No opposition from the air or ground

All fifteen B-17 bombers drop bombs together
In a train of bombs fifty feet apart
They hit the target straight on
Destroying a half mile stretch of tracks
Damaging the highway next to the tracks

The German army can't pass through this area
We continue flying south for five minutes
Over Normandy farmland
Then with hard right we turn west over the Atlantic Ocean
No flak over water

Then a right turn north and
Back to home base in Thorpe Abbotts
In time for a welcome GI dinner
All flyers know their task is accomplished
One more step toward the Allies recapturing France

We salute the Germen Army
And hope they have a good day
Running back to Germany

# MAQUIS MISSION

In the big B-17 Bomber
The co-pilot Captain Rosenthal
Hollered an order:
        "Navigator Lieutenant Knapp!
        Get up here quick!
        Climb into the pilot's seat!"
        Yes, sir!

He said, "Knapp, fly the plane!"
        So . . . I flew the plane!
Where were we headed
What were we doing
        Flying on a secret mission

The Maquisard French Resistance
        Needed help
Our 100th bomb group
        Was assigned a secret mission
        On French Bastille Day July 14, 1944

Twenty-seven B-17 bombers
        Loaded up with big parachuted canisters
        Packed with fighting supplies
        Flew in V formation, as a group
The Maquis needed help
        Our Flying-Fortresses were coming

Where were the French Maquis?
        Way south from our base in England
        In the central French mountains
        Waiting . . . waiting . . . waiting
For help from our Flying Fortresses

And here we came!
We were looking for three signal fires
	Burning on a field
	We saw them and the waiting GI trucks
And the waiting . . . waiting . . . waiting
Anxious Maquis

Flying very low just
	1200 feet above them
We dropped the parachuted canisters
	Jubilant French Maquis
	Had new weapons

But hold on
	Something was wrong with the plane
	What was that?
Chute cords were hung up
	One parachuted canister was caught
	Swinging just below our bomb bay

Our nervy Pilot Lieutenant Gilles
	Sprang up from his pilot's seat
Two gunners lowered him
	Head-first into the open bomb bay
	He began to cut the hung-up chute chords

A hung-up canister dropped into
	A surprised French farmer's barn yard
What would have happened
	If our Pilot had fallen out?
The Co-pilot and I would have flown
	Back to our English bomber base
	And landed that big bird

What would have happened?
If we got strafed by German fighters
        And the co-pilot had been hurt?
Could I have
        Landed our big bird alone?
You're dang right!

But our pilot hung on.
        They closed the bomb bay doors,
        Pilot Gilles climbed up into his seat.
I climbed back down into my seat.

Then our Pilot flew us back
        To our English bomber base.
He landed our big bird with a
        Beautiful landing.
I quit sweating.
        The crew quit sweating

We all had a new hero:
        Pilot Lieutenant W. Gilles!
And the French Maquis had new weapons
        To fight tyranny

**Strike photo of the Maquis Mission Signal Fires.** As our 100th group arrived deep in southern France, we spotted the Maquis signal fires, three fires in a triangle showing us the drop zone. This was our target for the day. We were there to parachute supply canisters into the center of the three signal fires. The Maquisards now had new equipment.

**Strike Photo of a Canister on Farmer's Roof.** As our pilot cut the snarled chute cords, the canister dropped onto a French farmer's roof. France's most surprised farmer. Let's hope he knew the Maquis!

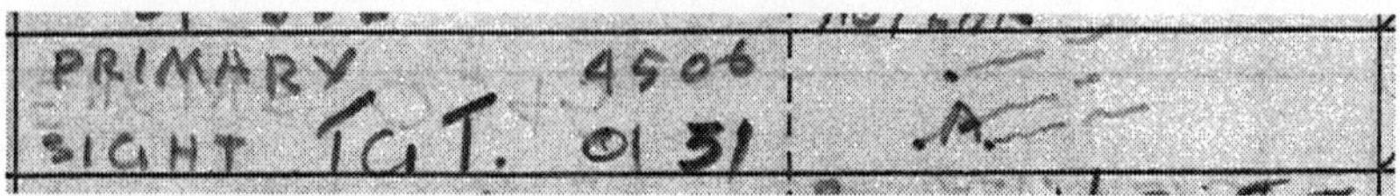


**Three Signal Fires in Navigator's Log.** The navigator is the one person on a combat crew who has pencil and paper. He records his observations in his navigator's log. My daughter found this notation of the signal fires while reading my log. This note shows that we reached our Primary target (A) to drop supplies for Maquis. I also made a drawing of the three signal fires we saw in the field. Incidentally most of the canisters hit the target and the French got new equipment. Viva la France!

# JOHN'S 28TH MISSION

I flew my 28th combat flying mission
On my 28th birthday
On July 28, 1944
I was a 1st Lieutenant Navigator

Because I was based in England
I knew the sensors would cut
My story from any letter
I mailed home

How could I get this story home
I talked to the Major in S-2 Intelligence
He knew how to beat
The system

The Major said,
"I know just what to do."
We'll send a news release
To your hometown newspaper

I'll write the news story while you
Have your photo taken in front of your B-17
Wear your parachute straps
Don't smile

Where does your family live
Where is your good wife living
What a story . . . the Detroit News
Will surely print it

Your family will see this story
In two days
They will get a dozen
Phone calls

Your wife will be delighted
To have a detailed story
From her dear husband

I felt like I was waving to Max
From across the Ocean
Happy reading, Max!

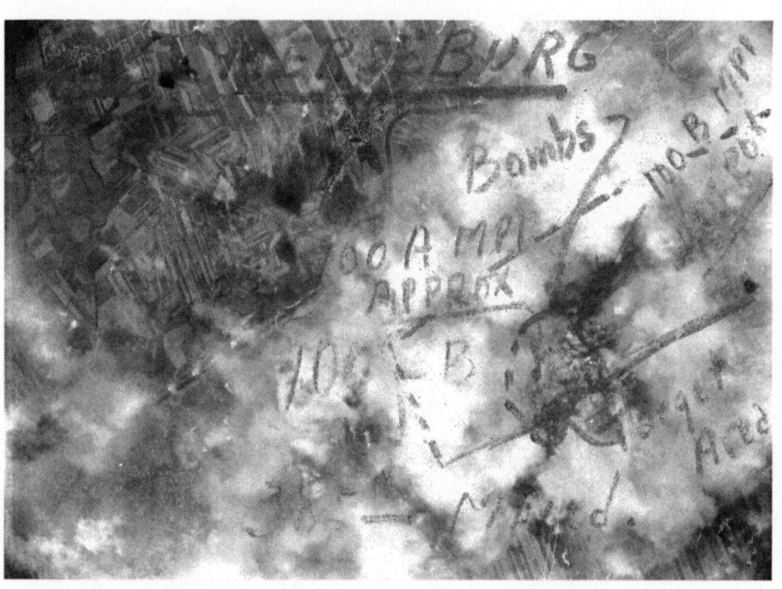


**Strike Photo of John's 28th Mission.** A strike photo is shot by an automatic camera in several lead planes. By studying of a series of strike photos the S-2 staff can make an assessment of the target's bomb damage. In this strike photo the Nazi fighter factory in Poland was demolished.

**John's 28th Mission Photo.** Lieutenant E. John Knapp, Navigator. On July 28, 1944, on his 28th birthday, John flew his 28th combat mission.

*City Brevities*

**28th Mission on 28th Birthday**—Lieut. Eliud J. Knapp, Fortress navigator ,flew his 28th mission over Germany on his 28th birthday on July 28. The next day he flew his 29th mission, then stayed on the ground for a day to let the numbers go by. A former student of architecture at Lawrence Institute of Technology here, Knapp is the son of Mr. and Mrs. Clifford H. Knapp, 9117 Woodrow Wilson avenue. His wife, Mrs. Ellen Maine Knapp, lives with his parents. Knapp is based in Britain.

Knapp

**John's 28th Mission Detroit News Article.** This is the story the Detroit News printed in 1944. This is what John's wife Max and my family found in their paper one day. They saved the clipping for me to see when I came home. I was surprised to see the photo they chose to use didn't show me in all my flying gear.

# FINAL 35TH MISSION

I was rousted out of bed at 3:30 a.m.
The Sergeant said, "Good morning.
You have a 2,780 gallon mission."
That meant we needed full gas tanks
For our B-17 on a long mission

I asked to be excused because
This was my 35$^{th}$ and final run and
I was wishful for a "Milk Run"
But no Navigators
Got excused from this long mission

At 4:30 a.m. in the S2 briefing room
We saw where Headquarters is sending our Group
The day's target was
Way beyond and east of Berlin, Germany
To a Posnan, Poland fighter plane factory
With at least thirteen hours of air time
"You're our good luck charm, John!
You always return!"
I shrug and say it's okay with me

This was not just a long mission
It was a long mission with no expected
Nazi fighter opposition
They hadn't figured out
Where we were going

We did face a lot of flak at the target
But our bombs demolished the
The Nazi fighter plane factory
Then we headed home
Wondering if the fighters would find us
On our return flight

I navigated us out over the Bering Sea
No flak guns surrounded us
No enemy fighters followed us

Our return flight was long
Six hours of routine formation flying
No GI food
No GI warm coffee
On GI oxygen all the way

Home base never looked better
Before landing the pilot flew
Around two sides of the landing runway and
Let me shoot my jubilant signal flares
I shot yellow flares for my final mission
(Red was an alert for wounded on board)

It was a good smooth landing
The pilot parked the plane and
The exhausted crew jumped out

I dropped my two briefcases
On the pavement below and
Climbed out of the plane
I tried to pick up both briefcases
But their weight pulled me down to the ground

Two gunners came over quickly
And picked me and my briefcases
Up off the ground
I was too exhausted to know it
The gunners had slept for several hours
No Nazi fighters to shoot at
But I had to work the whole thirteen hours

Our favorite Cook had
Hot cross buns and coffee
Waiting for us in the S2 debriefing room
My 35th Mission
My final combat flight was over

Now was the time for me to
Transfer to S2 Air Corps Intelligence
I looked forward to becoming
A ground pounder

**Strike Photo of 35th Mission.** The target was east of Berlin in Posnan, Poland. According to the S-2 officer's study and appraisal of these strike photos there were direct hits on this Nazi fighter factory. The majority of the bomb bursts are within the target area. All of the group's planes had direct hits. I was especially interested in seeing these strike photos to understand this long mission's results. By a chance of fate this was one of the longest combat missions I ever flew. This was my final combat mission—the 35th—to complete my flying tour of duty. Now I could transfer to S-2 Air Corps Intelligence staff.

Knowe alle men by yese presentes that ye

LUCKYE BASTARDES CLUB

A gatherynge of G.F.U's assembled in Grayte Brytagne

Do herebye admytte untoe theyre brotherhoode one Eliud N. Knapp

Who on thys 24th daye of Aug; Anno Domini 1944 hath acheyved to eminence by reasone of havinge sallied forthe no lesse than 35 tymes ande also bye Godde's Grace havinge returned inne safetie frome eache ande everye sallye – transporteing for ande unto ye German Reich full manye a tonne of petardes, mines, balles of fire ande othere greyvous burthens for ye discomfiting of ye manne Hitler ande alle his eville companye unto ye Glorie of Godde to whom be thanksgiveing for this deliveraunce. Albeit sayd 1st Lt. Knapp was fulle manye a tyme ande ofte sore affryghted bye reasone of ye manye pittefalles and snares sette before hym bye ye foe, yette did he on eache occasion returne untoe hys companye wyth linen unbesmirched ande a lightsome harte, cryinge forthe unto hys compagnons "C.S." whyche is to saye a milke runne.

Commanding Officer

Air Executive — Squadron C.O.

Official Seal — Group Operations — Squadron Operations

**Luckye Bastardes Club.** Whenever an airman completes a 35-mission tour he was introduced into this exclusive club known as "The Lucky Bastards." I got my certificate on August 24th, 1944. Of course this is a prized possession.

# CHAPTER #4

# S-2 Intelligence

# A DAY WITH S-2

I survived thirty-five combat missions
Then the Major recruited me
For S-2 Air Intelligence staff
My daily routine took a different direction

Now I had to roll out of a warm bed
At 3:30 not 4:30 a.m.
I had pre-flight work while
Flight crews were still sleeping

Quick! Shave, wash, dress, eat breakfast
Run to the S-2 briefing room
On secret red phone with Headquarters
Received the day's targets and flight routes

I prepared flight routes with strings
And the day's targets with pins
On a huge wall map of occupied Europe
Then I revealed the target to S-2 officers and briefed them

The staff prepared about fifty target packets
Of the day's targets and flight routes
Maps, target information, photos, flak sites

We met with squadron B-17 flight crews
Briefed navigators and bombardiers
With the day's targets and flight routes
Briefed navigators on radio signals for flight formation

The time for squadron takeoff was set
We knew what time our flyers
Would hit the English Channel coast
We knew what time they
Would hit their targets
We knew when to anticipate radio strike reports

So I drove a Jeep out to the end of
The long east-west runway
And counted the beautiful big
B-17 birds taking off
And forming up into squadrons

I knew what time our group flyers
Would return hours later
So I drove the jeep back to
The end of the runway

Waiting and waiting for the
Combat planes to return and
To count them
As they landed on our airstrip

After all flyers in squadron had returned
Crews were de-briefed by S-2
For combat and strike information
What the crews saw was collected and reported
For Intelligence information

Then the flight crews headed
Back to bed
For some needed sack time

In a hurry the Photo Staff
Removed strike cameras from
The returning planes to develop strike photos
Of each target hit that day

The strike photos were displayed
In the Group Library for navigators and bombardiers
To study and to learn

S-2 Intelligence staff received
Each day's mission strike photos
And interpreted for strategies
That may be useful for
The next day's combat mission

**S2 Intelligence Men.** The complete S-2 Intelligence staff. By showing this photo, I am giving recognition to these wonderful highly trained staff people. The S-2 staff dealt so much with military secrets that few people knew how big a staff the Bomb Group needed. I am seated 4th from the left.

**S-2 Briefing Room.** The S-2 crew briefing room shows a large map of Europe with the target of the day shown by white pins at target locations. The routes to the target locations were shown by red colored strings stretching from home base to target. This was the first indication the pilots and crews had of the day's combat mission's site location. The location of German flack guns were indicated with red circles showing the area and distance range the flack guns could shoot. The flying routes to targets were planned to avoid as many flack guns as possible.

**Combat Crew Library.** The 100th Bomb Group set up a Combat Crew Library. This photo shows many men very interested in their work. Any member of a combat crew could come to this room and study the results of the previous day's bombing mission. Strike photos of bombing hits and S-2 mission analysis papers were available for airmen to study.

**John Walking on Path.** I'm walking from the S-2 office to the gunner's briefing hall. The gunners received the same briefing for the day's targets and flack gun locations that the pilots are given.

# SOARING, SHOOTING & SINGING

What do combat flyers do
In between flying combat missions
When they are not dropping bombs
Or shooting at German fighters
Or being shot at with German flak

If we flew two missions each week
That left five days and nights with no assigned duty
Often we flew four combat missions a week
with three days in between to rest, loaf
And be idle in a stand-down

Major Bowman of S2 was a choir director in a church in Boston
He organized a men's choir on the 100th Bomb Base
He recruited a dozen men who liked to sing
This was the start of a really good singing group
We called ourselves the "100th Bomb Group Choir"

The 100th bomb base had a chapel
Occupied only on Sunday mornings
The Chaplin offered his okay
To the choir to practice there
The chapel had a piano but no organ

For us the chapel was the perfect place
To practice choir singing
One of the officers was the piano player
Attendance at choir practice was almost 100%
We practiced one day each week

We had three tenors, five baritones, and four bass singers
Who made a good balanced choir
More officers discovered us and wanted to join
Major accepted all those that could sing
As other voices were added we just got better

Some voices had choir experience
But most of us had a lot to learn
Major was a bug on attacks and releases in a song
We all learned plenty from him
As we say today—most of us had a steep learning curve

Soon more singers began to show up
One officer had a beautiful high tenor voice
A sergeant came to us with another tenor voice
That showed soprano qualities
We were excited with the quality of our choir's voices

Two GI sergeants in the choir
Wrote a song about the 100th Bomb Group
They took their composition to London
A music firm published their song
The entire choir learned the song

One summer weekend the Major took a railroad trip
To London to visit music stores
He purchased many sheets of music
Some of the sheet music he kept a secret
From the members of the choir

His well-kept secret came out in September
When he asked us if we would like to sing
The great music of Handel's "Messiah"
We were thrilled to sing this masterpiece of Christian music
We said, "May we practice more than once a week?"

The choir had about three months to learn
And practice this wonderful music
In order to present it in the 100th Base Chapel on Christmas
This became our 100th Bomb Group Choir's singing goal

The people in the little city of Diss near our Bomb Base
Found out about our 100th Bomb Group Choir
The local Episcopal Church invited us to sing the "Messiah"
With them in their ancient church
They had a fine organ, but few men to sing and no soprano

Our 100th Bomb Group piano player
Was thrilled to have the opportunity to play their organ
For our singing of Handel's "Messiah"
They promised us a good meal
After the singing concert

This ancient church had a bronze plaque
On the entry wall recording that the nave was built in 1206 A.D.
It was over 700 years old—built before America was discovered
The organ was rebuilt in 1876 A.D.
So was in good shape
For our presentation of the "Messiah"

Our 100th Bomb Group Choir Sing was a few days
Before Christmas in December 1944
We all knew we needed to sing our best performance
World War II was not over yet
But we had found hidden joy in this wartime experience

The choir's singing went very well as all of us wanted to bring
Some sense of inspiration to the wonderful English people
Who had invited us to sing in their ancient Episcopal Church
Our tenor sang the soprano parts of the "Messiah"
And lifted all of us in the choir and the congregation
To a higher level

After our presentation of the "Messiah"
The great solos and the beautiful organ music
The people ushered us into the Great Hall
To serve us a good meal
We were very surprised with the plentiful food
Served by the grateful people of Diss, England

We decided to thank the Diss congregation
By putting on an impromptu 100th Bomb Group Choir Sing
Naturally we sang "God Bless America"
And many English songs of the Royal Air Force
And the British Army and several American folk songs

You can imagine how well
Our spur-of-the-moment Choir Sing was received
We American men were pleased to experience a civilian event
And the English were pleased to experience an enriched Christmas experience
Shouting "Hurray for you, Yanks" and "Bravo, Bravo"

**Singing the Messiah** The 100th Bomb Group Choir singing Handel's Messiah for Christmas in the Diss EP church. Major Bowman is in the center directing the two choirs. I can be seen among the singers on the right.

**100th Choir in Church.** The 100th Bomb Group Choir singing Handel's Messiah for Christmas. This ancient early English Gothic church, 700 years old, is quite beautiful. The pipes of the old organ played by our musician can be seen up above the Choir. The Choir was inspired to sing this great music with these local English people in their ancient church structure. They made us Air Corps men feel welcome and we almost forgot the war for over an hour.

# RINGING IN DISS

The Rector from the Diss Episcopal Church
Favored the 100th Bomb Group Choir
With a special visit to his ancient Diss church

The church building had a high stone tower
With many bells of different sizes and tones
We climbed up two stories in the tower
To see the bell ringers

The bell ringers were two stories below the bell story floor
The local people rang these bells
By pulling on each bell's rope
To play a song

They rang Christmas bell music for us
We applauded the effort of our English hosts
Who were extending their gratitude to us Yanks
From the 100th Bomb Group Choir

# THE CALAIS MILK RUN

It's 3:30 a.m.
The sergeant woke me up
As a 35 mission navigator
I've been reassigned to S2 Air Intelligence
No longer flying combat
Now teaching and briefing gunners for flights

After D-Day our group
Hit targets in occupied Europe
Today's mission was special
So we were up early

In the breakfast dining room
All have questions on the day's mission
And why . . . who knows . . . no briefing yet

The three pre-flight briefing rooms
Will be busy this morning
I wondered what the mission was for the day
I headed to the S2 briefing room for targets and routes

The day's mission: Crossing the English Channel
To the French Calais coast
I ran to the gunners' briefing room
On the big map I set up red string routes and white pin targets

I pulled the stage curtain in front
And watched the gunners arrive
"Pay attention," I said. This is an important flight."
I pulled the curtain back to show mission routes

The room erupted with hollering
Gunners yelled, "This is a milk run!"
Milk run Milk run Hurray Hurray
My briefing told the gunners they would miss flak
Short time over land—long time over water

Direct flight route along French coast
Then half left turn to Calais coast
Direct flight in . . . drop bomb load
Quick U-turn out over the sea

Can this be a second D-Day landing site?
Pre-landing bombing
Who knows this time?
The target was a concentration of artillery
We expected no opposition from fighters or flak guns

The gunners were correct
It was a milk run
All the planes returned

De-briefing after landing
Gunners wanted to know why Calais
I didn't have any answer for them
"Ask the General."
A month later we all learned the target was
A secret weapons site
I was as glad to learn that as the gunners were

**Flag at Half-Mast.** President Roosevelt died in 1945 before WWII ended. The 100th Bomb Group and all USA service organizations lowered their flags to half-mast in the President's honor. This flag at half-mast is in front of the Group's Headquarters, in Thorpe Abbotts, England.

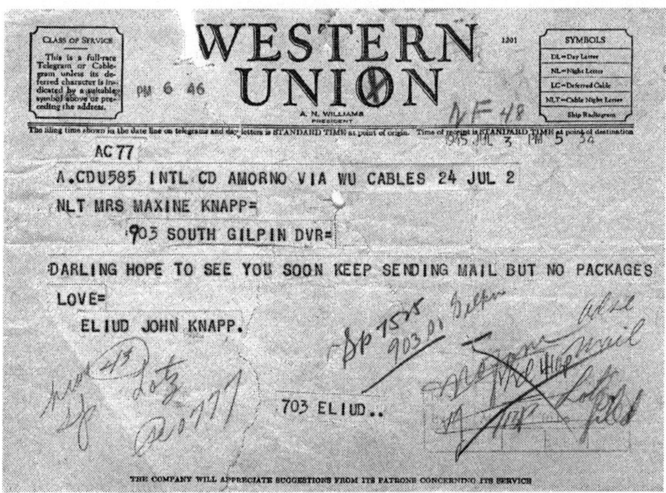

WESTERN UNION

A. N. WILLIAMS, PRESIDENT

CLASS OF SERVICE
This is a full-rate Telegram or Cablegram unless its deferred character is indicated by a suitable symbol above or preceding the address.

SYMBOLS
DL=Day Letter
NL=Night Letter
LC=Deferred Cable
NLT=Cable Night Letter
Ship Radiogram

PM 6 46

The filing time shown in the date line on telegrams and day letters is STANDARD TIME at point of origin. Time of receipt is STANDARD TIME at point of destination

1945 JUL 3 PM 5 34

AC77

A.CDU585 INTL CD AMORNO VIA WU CABLES 24 JUL 2

NLT MRS MAXINE KNAPP=

903 SOUTH GILPIN DVR=

DARLING HOPE TO SEE YOU SOON KEEP SENDING MAIL BUT NO PACKAGES

LOVE=

ELIUD JOHN KNAPP.

703 ELIUD..

THE COMPANY WILL APPRECIATE SUGGESTIONS FROM ITS PATRONS CONCERNING ITS SERVICE

**Western Union Telegram.** I couldn't tell Maxine I was coming home straight out so this is how I told her. WWII in Europe was over but the Pacific war was still going on. The censors were using their red pencils and sharp knives on our letters and telegrams.

I have the nicest sweetest, handsomest, and romantic husband in all the world. My thoughts are always with you, my dearest.

**A Letter from Maxine.** I could hardly wait to get home to my dear wife, Maxine. We'd been "he" and "she" for three years—separated by thousands of miles. Soon we would become "us," starting our future together, building the family we'd always wanted.

# CHAPTER #5

# Home in Post-War U.S.A.

# WATCHING, WAITING

Watching the flak bursts around
our flying fortress
So thick you could walk on it
Jumping from burst to burst
at 35,000 feet
The Nazis ground gunners did
not have our range today

Watching the mission numbers grow
from mission number "one" to
mission number "thirty-five"
Which means I would be walking
on Mother Earth
from now on

Walking with other
ground pounders each day
would be an
easy adjustment

Watching over a slow army reassignment
from combat navigator
to air corps intelligence officer
made my new assignment official

Briefing receptive gunners
on today's mission worked better
than walking on flak bursts

Watching the Nazis retreat
back to their defeated fatherland
Raised my hopes to see
my Motherland again soon

Now, walking the deck of a
large banana boat from Liverpool
across the Atlantic to New Jersey

Walking through twelve fiction books
while on the Alexander Lillington
Rocking back and forth, up and down
all the way, for days
through storms and sunshine
Then a long train ride to
Harrisburg, Pennsylvania made a surprising adventure

Walking on USA ground
in the Army's discharge system
seems endless
But now I can phone home
after almost three years

My mother's voice is
as delicious as
a glass of warm milk
My dad's voice is
as good as a
first steak burger in years
But my darling wife's voice is
to me as sweet as honey
and angel food cake

And now, she's coming
Walking towards me
the full length of
Harrisburg railroad station
She walks fast
My heart is pounding
I stop walking
breathing in
this wonderful scene

Watching, I wanted this picture
to live in my mind
in full
There's her being
coming, beautiful
Walking fast to me
now us!

She's the woman I love
I am the man she loves
The first hug needed to be
a long one
The kisses needed to be
endless
These years apart
Disappeared
Now we're walking
as ONE,
again

**Max and John visit Camp Hillandale.** One of the important experiences of my early life was teaching kids swimming in the summer at Camp Hillandale near Holly, Michigan. I loved the camp and visited soon after coming home after the war. The owners were long-term friends and mentors. This photo of my lovely wife Max and I was taken shortly after my return from England and shows "us" starting to believe that WWII is really over.

# WE RETURN

## The Flight

Maxine told me in 1994 that
We should visit Thorpe Abbotts, England
I need to see where all you WWII
Young flyers were living and flying combat
What were your living conditions

We found a tour for the 100th Bomb Group
They had two seats to England
Now Max will have answers to
Her many questions
We could almost afford the trip
So we signed up to go

We climbed into an airliner in Madison, Wisconsin
Bigger than a B-17 . . . faster and peaceful
We found the 100th Bomb Group tour men and wives
At Heathrow Airport in London
Seated and waiting for us
They told us no drinking fountains
Better buy some bottled water

## The Visit

The tour bus driver dressed in khaki told Max
We have arrived at Thorpe Abbotts
They set up chairs in front of the control tower
We were greeted with grateful prayer
By the Episcopal Rector next to the East-West runway

The **Control Tower** had been
Converted to a 100th Bomb Group Museum
Full of WWII memories
Including photos of B-17 crews
Max was impressed to tears

Someone said
Look up into the sky Max
A 100th Bomb Group B-17 was flying overhead
Bow your heads for a dedicated airman
Major John Bennett's ashes were strewn out from the B-17
And returned to his base and Mother Earth

**To Rest**

Max asked me where is the airmen's cemetery
The tour bus driver wearing a brown sweater
Answered please get in the bus folks
I will take you there

We arrived at Cambridge to visit the
USA Air Corps Cemetery which had hundreds of crosses
All of the 100th Bomb Group graves were marked with flags
We found several flying buddies' graves
Max and I stood quietly and honored each with prayer

**Chapel at rest**

Max asked the bus driver as he removed his hat
Where on English soil did
The US Air Corps and the Royal Air Force
Construct an honorary chapel to airmen
He informed us, you can't miss it
It's in Cambridge Cemetery

We thanked the smiling bus driver
For directing us to the beautiful chapel
Which honored and remembered many American flyers
Who came to English land
Fighting for freedom from our common enemy

## Church

The next day was Sunday
Attending church sounded good
Our driver told Max he was driving the tour group to
Thorpe Abbotts All Saints Episcopal Church
An ancient church built with local flint fieldstone

We were not prepared for what happened next
The long sidewalk to the church was lined with
British veterans greeting us
With smiles handshakes and gratitude to us Yanks
Max and I and the other tour members
Were overwhelmed by these wonderful British vets

The church service and hymns we sang were uplifting
We especially enjoyed the
Rector's sermon
Couched toward us Yanks

After the church service a local lady showed us the
Church window dedicated to the many
U.S. Airmen who fought and died while
Participating in the saving of England in WWII
And the people of Thorpe Abbotts knew it

Yanks are not accustomed to being honored this way
Many quiet tears were shed by
Flyers their wives and tour friends
We felt the strength of British character

## Air Museum

The British designed excellent war aeroplanes
The bus driver drove us to the
Duxford Aeroplane Museum where we saw
Many old and new British fighting aeroplanes

At the aerodrome outside the museum
Several men of the tour group
Spotted a British Spitfire WWII fighter plane
The pilot was showing off to his lady
Flying her aloft in a wonderful aeroplane

## Shakespeare

Maxine wanted to know what
Shakespeare's home was like
So we found out in Stratford-on-Avon

Beautiful English flower garden
A roof of grass called thatch
Walls of plaster and timbers
Wind-leaky doors and small rain-leaky windows
Floors of soil and house heated by fireplace

Meals cooked in a wood-burning fireplace
People ate their meals at a plank table
Seated on wood stools
Wooden forks and spoons

Max and I stayed at the Moat House Hotel
Stratford-on-Avon, Warwickshire
On the Fourth of July, 1994
No Independence Day celebrations in England

We ate lunch at the Black Swan Inn
That the WWII GIs had nicknamed the Dirty Duck
Max found me an electric razor part at a chemist shop
And it fit

## Cathedral

The tour guide included a trip
To the great Norwich Cathedral
A boy's choir greeted us with a concert of
Uplifting English chorale music
In the courtyard outside the cathedral

An old example of English Vertical Gothic
Not damaged in WWII
We were guided throughout the Cathedral
The interior nave was awesome over 100 feet high
Built of English limestone
Still an active institution in Norwich

## Book

I was writing a book in my spare time in England
On architectural planning
By my great luck a friend from S2 Intelligence
A journalist professor from Princeton
Sat with me in the hotel lobby and critiqued my book
What a joy! What a help!

**We Return to the USA**

On the sixth morning the English bus driver
Loaded us and our luggage aboard
Along with great memories
Drove us back to Heathrow Airport in London

As we rode along in the bus
To return home to the USA
The thought kept coming back to me
Where is my ten-man B-17 crew today
Sixty-five years later
I am STILL WAITING for their flight's return
From their ill-fated mission of 1944

**British Church dedication to USA flyers.** On our return trip to Thorpe Abbots in April of 1994 we discovered this English generation was full of gratitude towards the many men of the 100th Bomb Group. In the Thorpe Abbots EP Church we found a door dedicated to the airman of the 100th Group. The women of the church explained their gratitude and why they had this door made in our honor.

**Control Tower Museum.** After the 100th bomb group left England for the USA the grateful English people decided to convert the control tower to a museum. Many veterans contributed money and uniforms and other memorable items to the museum. In 1994 a group of us 100th Bomb Group veterans from America paid the Thorpe Abbotts museum a visit. We were all inspired and grateful to these thoughtful people for their efforts. This was a wonderful honor we will never forget.

**John Visits Cambridge Cemetery.** All my photos from our return trip to England were lost. This is a scan of the only one we saved. We located some of the graves of the 100th bomb Group flight crews. I am standing by a cross of one of the 100th Bomb Group identified by flags for us by the cemetery management.

# CELEBRATE WWII VETERANS HONOR FLIGHT

06/16/09

We came
We walked with a cane
We walked with a walker
Some seated in wheel chairs
We came standing tall
We Missouri Veterans of WWII

We came from
Fayette, Fulton, Eldon and Ewing
from Jamestown, Jefferson City
and Bowling Green
From Holt Summit and Moberly
We all came to Columbia, Missouri to join
our Comrades in arms
of sixty-five years ago

We gathered in Columbia
All headed to the Missouri Honor Flight
in Washington, D.C.
To experience the WWII Memorial

We departed from the hotel lobby
Headed for the big bus to St. Louis Airport
We encountered a large noisy crowd
of patriots at 3:30 a.m.

They waved Old Glory and
Yelled, "Thank you! Thank you,
Vets for your service to our country!"
We never saw such gratitude before
Few dry eyes got on the bus

American people want to show
Respect to American veterans
But opportunities are few for that expression
This trip gave many people the chance
To express gratitude to us

We departed on our two-hour flight
This squadron of excited vets
We marched into the Baltimore Airport terminal
To a large crowd of Americans
Who found their way to salute and thank
Us visiting WWII vets

The terminal gate was lined with
A dedicated troop of Boy Scouts
And many grateful American citizens
All yelling, "Thank you! Thank you!"
All applauding loudly
For the service we veterans gave to
Our freedom country

There never was any doubt
In the minds of us WWII vets
But now we experienced
Adulation and gratitude first-hand
From grateful American people
And we were overcome

At the end of the long day
Riding in the bus toward home
A wonderful convoy of light blossomed
As a state trooper leading our bus
Pulled slightly ahead and
The road space was filled with
The Patriot Motor Bike group

The bikers saluted the Veterans
By flashing their tail lights
Red white and yellow blinking lights
In a beautiful half mile of tribute

We vets saw the flashing lights
We vets "GOT IT"
So we clapped and yelled
Hoping the bikers were hearing us
Thank you bikers for a
Beautiful display of patriotic gratitude
We vets of WWII loved it

**Bikers Saluting the Veterans.** This is a dark night photo, but I felt it should be here because we all appreciated the bikers so much.

# WWII MEMORIAL

We arrived walking tall
We arrived tapping a cane
We arrived pushing a walker
We arrived in a wheel chair

We are brothers sisters aunts uncles
Neighbors friends and many others
We are comrades and vets of WWII from Missouri

We arrived experiencing the WWII Memorial
We came to see the victory memorial
On the Washington, D.C. mall

We arrived seeing the memorial
To our efforts
And we arrived seeing the memorial to
Our comrades who fell in battle

They arrived by memory with us
We feel their presence standing with us
Thank you USA for remembering them

We saw many stone towers
Memorials for each state
Proud to find the state of Missouri
Proud to find Michigan state of my birth

We saw the large pool of the waters
For Pacific and Atlantic theaters of combat
Looking down the reflecting pool mall
We felt that the country today
Values the efforts of veterans

We appreciated the bronze eagles
Reflecting the pride all vets feel
Now I feel it and can say it
"I am proud be an
American veteran."

**John visits the WWII Memorial**. The Mid-Missouri Honor Flight is a volunteer group. They send WWII Veterans to Washington, D.C. at no cost to them. This is a wonderful opportunity for these Vets to see and walk around in the WWII Memorial Monument built on the Capitol Mall for the Veterans who performed for our country. Here I'm standing next to the Michigan monument. I'm thinking about the crew I lost in the war.

# MY FLAG FLIES

My flag comes out of
        the closet.
The dust is snapped off
        the colored fabric.
The two-piece flagpole
        fits tight again.

I peek out
        the front door,
And look up and down
        my street.
I see five neighbors'
        flags flying.

My flagpole comes out
of my hands and into
the flag bracket.
        It fits.
        My flag flies.
        It is snapping in the wind.

My flag flying says to
        my neighbors' flags,
"Can you answer
        with snapping
in the wind?"

They all answer,
proclaiming their color.
        by snapping stripes and stars.
All flags in this block
        love to be snapping
        with the wind.

My immigrant neighbors' flags
all snap together.
Coming together from five countries.
Proclaiming their color.
By snapping together.
As my flag flies.

**My Flag Flies.** If you look closely, you can see I have a small flag tucked in the back of my Thorpe Abbotts cap.

We arrived walking tall
We are comrades and vets of WWII from Missouri
We came to see the victory memorial
On the Washington, D.C. malls
And we arrived seeing the memorial to
Our comrades who fell in battle

# CHAPTER 6

# The Family Grows

# REMEMBERING MOM'S DAY

A poem to my children in 1995

What does your Dad say on a Mother's day? (Post WWII)
Perhaps I should say
For me it's gratitude.
Gratitude for many things,
for life alive
for people,
for our Family,
for friends,
for relatives,
for neighbors,
Who we may say?
This is the easiest answer of the day,
especially on Mom's Day.

**Chapter 1**
We were grateful for the first child
In our Family.
We both wanted a girl child.
Picked out both a girl child's name,
(M for Maxine and J for John)
Marcia Jane
Plus a boy child's name
(M for Maxine and J for John)
Michael John
just to be safe.

Dad shouted over the phone to his Mom
**"It's a girl!"**
A beautiful little girl child,
named Marcia Jane
and MOM was very happy.
That's a shout of gratitude.
We were fulfilled.

**Chapter 2**

Your MOM wanted a girl child again.
So that's what we ordered.
for our Family.
We picked out a girl child's name,
Laura Susan
(Laura for a friend and Susan for Max's Mother)
and remembered the unused boy's name,
Michael John
(M for Maxine and J for John)

The relatives and friends said,
"It will be a boy child!"
Did we pray for a girl child again?
Of course,
but we knew the Lord might
send a boy,
and we were ready.
Again we were grateful
Your MOM was full of gratitude.
She looked very full of gratitude!
Your Dad kept telling your MOM,
"Expect a girl child."

Came the big shout over the phone this time.
**"It's the girl child Max wanted!"**
On time,
on schedule,
as ordered,
a lovely little girl child,
named Laura Susan
And we forgot about the boy child's name!

**Chapter 3**

The entire neighborhood told your MOM,
"If you have two girls, then
the third will surely be a girl child, too!"
We only thought of a new
Boy child's name,
for our Family,
for that's what your
MOM wanted.

Gratitude is powerful and a good idea, too.
We looked for one new name for
this favorite son of your MOM.
Or should we say, for a powerful three?
E. J. Knapp, the third!
E. John Knapp, the second!
Eric John Knapp, the first!
Sounded good and rang of gratitude,
For our idea of a Family.

This time it wasn't a shout over the phone,
It was a big yell!
**"It's the boy child Max wanted!"**
The two girls and
The dad and mom, all,
We cried with joy.
And we laughed with joy.
And we cried with gratitude.
And we laughed with gratitude
for the boy child
named Eric John.
The whole Family jumped for joy,
Grandma, Grandpa,
Aunts, Uncles,
Brothers, Sisters,
And the neighbors, all
jumped for joy.
Mom had her three!
These were her family.

**And these are my thoughts on MOM'S Day.**
for our Family is now complete,
And these are the words
I want to say
on MOM'S day.
And this is my prayer of gratitude I give
on MOM'S day.
I'm grateful for
my children,
my family,
and my good neighbors.
So, tell me what are your thoughts of gratitude,
And your words of gratitude?
on MOM'S Day.

This Dad may already know!

*Ellen Maxine Gleason Knapp*
*August 8, 1918–March 8, 1996*

**The Five of Us.** I'm standing next to my beloved wife, Maxine. Seated, our three wonderful children: Laura, Eric, and Marcia. (L-R)

# A CHRISTMAS TALE OF FAITH AND REALIZATION: FOR THE YEARS 1941 TO 1995

A post WWII CHRISTMAS poem by E. John Knapp

Once upon a time
a long time ago,
a young man called John and
a young women called Maxine
got married after a very short courtship.
They both found the Love
they were looking for.
And it was very, very good.

Shortly they settled into
their apartment.
And
the Big Stupid War broke out.
The young man called John
was called into the Air Corps.
The young woman called Maxine
did not think this was very good.
The young man called John
Did not think this was very good.

Within a short time,
Lieutenant John was flying overseas,
navigating a big bird, B17 bomber.
Lieutenant John flew many missions,
dropping bombs on
European Nazi war machine

Many buddies were shot
out of the skies.
One day the commanding officer
Said, "Lieutenant, you *will* ***not*** *fly* with your crew today."
No reason given.
So he stayed grounded that day.
This was not felt to be very good.

The fortunes of war fated
this day
his crew
without their navigator was
shot down
over Normandy in France.

Lieutenant John did not know how to
let his pretty wife know
he was not on the fateful mission.
He sent her a telegram,
saying "All is well."
Army censors let it go, and
she got the message.
He had been grounded this day.
This was not totally good.

From that day
Lieutenant John decided to pray
That the big stupid war
would end, and
then all of us would go home to
raise wonderful families.
He knew he had a
wonderful wife and
a superb marriage.
This could be very good.

After Lieutenant John completed a
35 mission tour,
and then served in
S2 Air Intelligence
The fighting stopped.
The big stupid WWII ended.
And this was very good.

Then Lieutenant John
came home.
Alive,
well,
with
no knowledge of
his flight crew's fate.
This was not totally good.

How do you tell
when a war
is over?
Fighting stops.
Fighting men and women
come home,

but the price of this big stupid encounter,
is what will happen to the lives of
All the people and
all the fighting men and women.
How can
they get
their lives back together?
and have very good lives?

The Lieutenant noted his prayers
were answered.
His life continued into
the next phase.
His daily prayers were
to realize how
wonderful home is,
his wonderful marriage, and
raising a wonderful family would be.

The Lord smiled upon him and his wife.
Came the miracle of
a newborn child.
John looked down
upon the
most beautiful girl child
in the world.
The great fact was
THE BIG STUPID WAR WAS OVER.
And this was a very, very good idea.

Do children realize the place they
have in the lives of others?
Do they understand the
importance of
their position in
the family ?
This first child, a girl, had a
triple importance:
John was alive,
Maxine was alive,
The child was alive

and kicking.

This new family was a
continual reminder
of what the
word FAMILY means.
And this was very good.

So this Christmas season is a season of Joy:
A season of Joy:
for our family and for
three of the
most marvelous children
and five super
grandchildren,
The Lord has ever welcomed into
His Kingdom.
And this is continuously very good.

Note: I now have eight great-grandchildren and four more I also consider my great-grandchildren. I have everything.—November 2009

**John and Family at 90th birthday.** My marvelous family celebrated my 90th birthday on July 28, 2006 in northern Wisconsin at my daughter Laura's home on Lake Yawkey. They all understood that Grandpa John survived World War II and came home. Sixty years later, this is my family. Since this photo was taken, four more great grandchildren have joined the family and more are on the way.

# CHAPTER #7

# JOHN'S STORY

By Amy Wagner Knapp
—my daughter-in-law

## John's Story

by Amy Wagner Knapp, my daughter-in-law
12/16/05

"YOU'RE NOT GOING," THE NEW COMMANDER SAID, pointing at him. "Go in the other room."

"OK. Yes, Sir." Lieutenant Knapp had scarcely stepped into the busy briefing room before he was turning around and leaving again.

It was April 28, 1944, 02:00 hours. The crew of the Denver Doll was assembling for their preflight briefing along with the crews of eleven other B-17s in the 8th Army Air Force, 100th Bomb Group (Heavy), 349th Bomb Squadron, in Thorpe Abbotts, England.

First Lieutenant E. John Knapp, navigator, did not ask why he was pulled from the mission. He did not feel anger or disappointment or relief or anything else at all at being grounded. He was given an order, and he followed it. Emotions were not a part of life in the U.S. Army Air Corps. There was only the job to be done.

He stepped into the next room, out of sight and sound of Colonel Robert H. Kelly and the officers' briefing. The familiar map of Europe hung on the wall, dotted with colored pins and slips of paper marking targets, delineating missions. The room was dim, and the white walls looked yellow in the limited light of those early hours. Lieutenant Knapp knew that without himself as navigator, the bombardier, Second Lieutenant John M. Jones, would be taking his place. He marked some flight maps, hoping to explain the finer points of navigation to the bombardier, whom Lieutenant Knapp believed knew little about it.

Following the briefing, Knapp nabbed Jones as the officers left the briefing room to give some quick words of advice, then went back to bed as his crew left on their mission to Sottevast to destroy Nazi defenses.

Five hours later, Lieutenant Knapp awoke to the scuffling sounds of a young GI sweeping out the barracks. The officers occupying these barracks had hired an enlisted man to be their butler.

He swept the floors, polished boots, made the beds, and did anything else he was asked to. His domestic chores doubled his income. He was eager and chipper.

The sun peeked through the windows of the concrete hut. Seeing the light of day, Knapp was on his feet in a shot.

"What time is it?" he asked, pressing his thick, short hair into regulation order.

"0900, sir." The GI butler smiled and nodded. "They'll be getting back soon, sir," he said, turning back to his sweeping.

Knapp laced his boots and left his cot unmade. He made his way across camp, over the dry, packed, dirt roads, past row after row of huts, past young men going about their business, the business of war.

The building was bustling. None of the planes had returned yet, and the staff and S-2, Army intelligence, were buzzing. Men were busy with phones and papers, their words were hard, fast, and serious.

Knapp poured himself a cup of coffee and took a fresh, steaming cinnamon roll from the table. The air crews lived daily with the knowledge they might never come back, but those cinnamon rolls were one little incentive to return from every mission. I'll bet they don't get these in the infantry, he thought, allowing the heat and sweet to fill his mouth and warm his throat.

"Should be any time now," a gravelly voice said next to him.

Knapp turned to the man and nodded. His hat was askew and his jacket was unbuttoned. Lieutenant Markham was a navigator for another crew. "You're stuck here, too," Knapp said, eyeing him up and down, noting how similar they were in appearance.

"Yeah. Colonel Kelly's trying to leave his mark as our new commander." Markham rolled his eyes. "Nine days into the job, mind you. Thinks he's slicker than snot." He chortled. "Bit of a tosser, if you ask me."

Knapp laughed heartily, and his eyes sparkled. "Colonel Cluck-Cluck." He chuckled at his insubordination. He glanced at the clock on the wall.

Really, it was getting a bit late. He noted the quickness in the talk, the shifting of legs, the tension.

The minutes dragged. He paced. He chatted. He couldn't stand it.

He put his coffee cup on a wheeled cart against the wall. "I don't like this," he muttered to no one.

At 1000 hours, he left the building and grabbed a Jeep. He drove along the dirt road past Thorpe Wood, and turned toward the hardstands of the 349h squadron. Planes sat cold and idle, waiting, while others were being checked for the day's missions. He drove past the farm fields just opposite the base and west along the service road, past the control tower, to the end of his squadron's runway. He pulled the Jeep off the road and killed the engine.

Lieutenant Knapp waited at the end of the runway for his crew to return to Thorpe Abbotts. He watched the sky, the same blue sky that covered Denver, where his wife, Maxine, would still be sleeping, the same blue sky that covered Germany, where the Nazis would most definitely not be sleeping.

The runway was concrete, two feet thick, stuck in the middle of farm country in East Anglia. A row of short trees and hedges grew to the north, a buffer between the rural road, serving the farmers with their quaint thatched-roof cottages, and the military operation, serving the Americans' 100th Bomb Group.

Thorpe Abbotts, Norfolk, had more cows than people before the Americans arrived. The soldiers filled churches, pubs, and dance halls, and filled the young ladies' arms, whose own men were off serving in the war in Europe, Africa, and Asia. The Americans rode battered bicycles into country towns and rode trains into the big cities where they traded their rations of cigarettes for pints and steak dinners.

Lieutenant Knapp waited. The sun crept across the sky. Half an hour later, the bombers began to return. Knapp counted as he watched them pass over his head (one, two, three).

He heard their engines scream on descent (four, five), heard their tires screeching on the concrete (six, seven). He smelled the fumes of their spent fuel (eight, nine). He felt his chest and guts rattle and burn as they tore past him down the runway (ten). Ten. He counted ten. Not twelve. There should be twelve, he thought.

He waited. No sign of the Denver Doll.

He waited. Where are they?

Only ten planes. No Denver Doll.

He waited. He worried.

"Where are they?!" he shouted to the sun.

He waited. He worried. He knew.

Another Jeep pulled up beside him. Staff Sergeant Parrish Reynolds called to him.

"Your crew went down."

The men looked at each other.

First Lieutenant E. John Knapp cleared his throat and held his gaze. "How many chutes?" he asked.

"Three," Reynolds answered. Three POWs. Seven dead. Reynolds swallowed and looked at the steering wheel of his Jeep.

Knapp nodded, and Reynolds drove off.

Knapp coughed and spit. He put his hands on his hips and stared into the midday sun. Emotions were not a part of life in the U.S. Army Air Corps. He tried not to cry.

He clambered back into the Jeep and returned to the briefing room to find out what had gone wrong.

MAXINE KNAPP WAS A PETITE WOMAN. She was trim and short, ninety pounds soaking wet, John had said, and five feet tall exactly. Her face was the map of Ireland.

She had raven hair, shiny and thick with curls, which she kept off her face. Her skin was milk-white and smooth, and on her long lips she wore the dark red lipstick which was so fashionable during the war. Her eyes were clear, light blue, almond-shaped. Her legs were shapely, and she didn't mind showing them. She was beautiful.

Maxine had a vibrant personality and made friends everywhere she went. She was a sucker for slapstick humor and had an easy laugh, although she had no understanding of sarcasm. She had a kind heart and a strong work ethic. She would do anything to help someone in need.

Her parents had been sharecroppers in Arkansas. Poor dirt farmers, she always said. Her mother died when she was six, her father when she was seven. She lived with her older sister until her older brother, Eldon Gleason, reached majority at 21. At that, she moved to Seattle to live with him. It was not a good move. Her brother's young wife, Esther, resented Maxine, feeling that Eldon paid too much attention to her. She was physically, verbally, and emotionally abusive toward the girl, and eventually Maxine moved to Detroit, where her sister Harriet had settled with her new husband, Will. Her youth was spent in poverty, shuffling from one place to the next. She craved security.

She decided to make her own security by becoming self-reliant and self-supporting. To that end, as a young woman, she enrolled in business college, learning bookkeeping and accounting. She was happy to be able to take care of herself, but after a lifetime of uncertainty, those worries and doubts made their way into her thoughts constantly.

In 1940, she met John Knapp, a handsome, hard-working student of architectural engineering. The two were smitten instantly. "This is it!" she told her sister. John and Maxine married the following August. She felt happy and settled at last.

Less than a year into the marriage, John enlisted in the Army, and in 1943 he completed the Army Air Corps Navigation School in Monroe, Louisiana. Maxine understood his decision to join up. She accepted that it was the right thing to do for the country and the world. But security was not a part of life in the U.S. Army Air Corps.

When John shipped off overseas, Maxine moved to Denver to live with another Army wife. She shared an apartment with Lou McGuire, the wife of John's pilot, Jim McGuire, and their small daughter, Janey. They enjoyed each other's company and were glad to be with someone who shared the experience of having her husband flying combat missions over Europe. In Denver, Maxine found a job as a bookkeeper at the Internal Revenue Service.

The morning of Friday, April 28, 1944 began much like any other. Maxine arose and prepared breakfast for Lou and herself. She hustled about, getting ready for work, double-checking the stove, putting the dishes away, and doting on young Janey. Maxine was compulsively neat and would not leave the house until she was satisfied that it was truly clean. Pleased, she was putting on her long gloves when the doorbell buzzed.

She shot a glance at Lou. It was very early for someone to call. She set her purse beside the rocker in the small living room. She held her head high and answered the door.

A neatly dressed youth stood before her in his brown uniform. "Telegram for Mrs. McGuire."

Maxine looked at Lou, who had crossed the room upon seeing the boy with the telegram.

Lou took the telegram and looked at it. "MIA," she cried.

Maxine's stomach was in knots. She looked from Lou to the boy. "Well, where's mine?" she asked him. She crooked her head sideways a little.

"There's just the one, ma'am," he answered. He waited for his tip.

Lou sat down in the rocker and sobbed. She crumpled the telegram in her hand and rocked.

Janey walked to her and touched her cheek. "Mama crying?" she asked.

Maxine wrinkled her forehead. "But are you sure there's just one?"

The boy nodded. "Yes, ma'am," he said. He frowned and opened his mouth as if to speak, but stopped and said nothing.

"Oh," Maxine sighed. She reached into her purse for some change and gave it to the messenger. She clicked the door closed. Her telegram must have been delayed, she thought. John and Jim flew together. If one went down, so did the other.

Maxine went to Lou and Janey. They cried and hugged each other tightly, pulling on each other's dresses, clutching each other. Their greatest fear stared them straight in the face. John and Jim were dead. The two ladies looked at each other, devastated.

MIA—missing in action—everyone knew that MIA was the same as KIA, they just hadn't found the bodies yet to call them killed in action.

But Maxine hadn't gotten a telegram.

Maxine stood up and arranged herself again. "Well, it's just a matter of time before I get mine," she said.

Lou held Janey close and heaved a great breath. Janey was too young to understand. Lou looked into Janey's face and saw her dead husband looking back at her, the narrow little head, the pointed chin, the sticking-out ears, those thin eyebrows. Jim loved his country and he loved his God and he loved this child who would grow up with only stories of her father.

"In the briefing, Colonel Kelly told us that if we ran into flak on the bomb run, not to take evasive action. He said it ruined the bombardier's aim. Explained it like we were little kids, like he's an expert, and not even been on a mission yet.

"He musta read that in a book." Second Lieutenant Edgar Wolf was a pilot flying last in formation on the Sottevast mission. He had a big nose and thick lips. His hair was coarse and dark. He looked older than his 26 years, but then, all the men looked older than they were. "We were all cheering at our good luck getting such an easy milk run. We'd be over land hardly a few minutes. The briefing officer said only eight guns would be able to reach us." He almost chuckled, but he blinked it back.

Lieutenant Knapp stood with his arms crossed, listening to what had happened on the mission for which he stayed on the ground.

Wolf continued eagerly. "So we made our run over the target. But there were low clouds. 'Hold your bombs, we're going around again,' Kelly says. The great oaf. We musta made the longest 360-degree turn in recorded history. He took us way out over the water. Took forever. So we flew back in over the target. Same speed, same heading, same altitude—22,000 feet. He had us in rigid formation, by the book, you know. The Krauts, they got us good. Set their shells after that first run, and they were ready for us." He leaned back in his chair and blew out his breath. He nodded his big head up and down a few times. He squinted at the men crowded around him.

They coughed and hooted and shook their heads as he spoke. Knapp looked at the floor and shifted his weight.

Wolf took a big slug of coffee. He'd already had three or four cinnamon rolls. He deserved every morsel, he said, and they deserved two mission credits for that calamitous fiasco in the sky. "Colonel Kelly took a hit, and they just disappeared in all the flak and dust. I saw five chutes after, though. His wing ship went down, too. That was McGuire's plane. Took a hit to the left wing. Three chutes. They started to spin and dive and then they exploded. Bits of B-17 all over the place."

Knapp wondered who made it out. He was surprised anyone had.

A plane with one wing would have spun so fast that the centrifugal force would have trapped them all inside. Added to that, the left wing held a huge fuel tank, which surely explained the explosion.

Colonel Kelly left his mark, all right. Thirteen dead on his first mission, maybe even himself. Nothing to write home about.

Write home!

Maxine!

Knapp dashed out the door, running out of the administration site, up the road to the communications office. The sun was already low in the west, and the office door was darkly shadowed.

He burst inside. The door banged behind him, and the mousy com officer grimaced at him.

"I have to telegram my wife," Knapp panted.

The man at the desk was accustomed to desperate men who needed a telegram sent home immediately. "What's the emergency?" he asked, barely bothering to look up.

"She thinks I'm dead!" Knapp hollered. "You will have sent the telegram to McGuire's wife already. I have to tell her I wasn't on the mission!" He stood over the officer, who simply snorted.

"You know you can't tell her anything about your mission. It'll never pass the censor." He wobbled his head around like a chicken.

Knapp widened his eyes to thoroughly take in this yak of a human. "So I won't tell her about the mission! I'll just say, 'I'm OK.' How's that?"

"Well, you can tell her you're having a great time and you wish she were here, if you feel like it. Just lay off the mission."

Knapp shook his head and muttered. "Fine. Let's just do it."

The communications officer looked him over. "Mmhmm," he chirped.

Together they composed a harmless but meaningful telegram.

"She'll get it in a couple hours," the com officer said gently. "She'll get it! Don't worry."

"OK," Knapp said, relaxing. "OK." He just had to tell her he was OK. She needed to know. Maxine was the only thing in the world that mattered.

Maxine and Lou milled around their apartment. Little Janey was as cheerful as ever, her round, brown eyes alight.

The two women fussed in the kitchen, stared out the windows, patted the girl on the head. They cried. They wandered around.

Lou had started the task of calling people to tell them about Jim being MIA. She also called the other wives from the aircrew. They'd all gotten their telegrams.

Maxine was still waiting for hers. She couldn't imagine what was taking so long. The anxiety of waiting for a slip of paper to confirm what her guts told her—that John was MIA with the others—was making her ill.

She couldn't possibly drink another glass of water or warm milk, but there was Lou with a tray.

"Maybe John didn't go on the mission, Maxine," Lou reassured her. Neither of them believed it. She was sweet, even through her own horrible grief.

Maxine paced and twisted her fingers. "Well, why wouldn't he be on the mission?"

Lou leaned into the only soft chair in the apartment. "You know they can be grounded for any little thing. Maybe he had a cold or an ear infection."

Maxine didn't want to hope. It would be too hard when that telegram finally came to be crushed again. Her mind knew that there were no guarantees, that there were no real assurances; there was no such thing as security. She'd had that proven to her when she was orphaned at age seven. She had hoped when she got married that it was for good, forever. But then there was the Big Stupid War, and John became a flight officer. Waiting for that telegram was all part of the deal.

Still, she hoped anyway. And she prayed.

The doorbell buzzed again. Terror, resignation, and grief coursed through Maxine's soul. And hope. Hope was there, too. But she didn't believe it.

She straightened her hair. She felt silly for doing it, and it made her laugh and cry in a nervous yelp. She didn't look at Lou, who was watching her closely.

Janey bounded for the door. Lou intercepted her and pulled her to her hip.

Maxine gripped the doorknob hard and took a shallow breath. She pulled the door open and pasted a fake smile on her face.

The messenger stood before her. He wore the same crisp, brown uniform as the earlier messenger had, but it was a different boy. He smiled at her. He had a bright face without a trace of puberty.

"Telegram, missus," he said, proudly extending his hand. It must have been his first job.

So here it was. The little scrap that would change everything.

Maxine didn't even close the door before she read it: "All is well. Love, John."

Maxine screeched and collapsed onto the floor. Tears flew out of her eyes, hot and huge. "He's alive! He's alive! John's alive! He's alive!" She bawled into her hands. She laughed, giddy from shock. Relief and euphoria gushed out in sobs and blubbers.

Lou took the telegram and read it; she fell onto the floor with Maxine. She held her, happy and relieved for her friend. The two of them stayed on the floor, immobilized by emotion. One woman mourned the death of her husband, the other rejoiced in the life of hers.

First Lieutenant E. John Knapp flew 35 missions over Europe. On August, 24, 1944, he completed his tour and transferred to S-2, where he remained until the end of the war in Europe, May 1945.

Shortly after Jim McGuire's death, Maxine moved back to Detroit to live with John's parents and wait out the war for him there.

Knapp returned to the States in a banana boat. They docked in Harrisburg, Pennsylvania. He called Maxine as soon as he stepped onto land.

She got on the first train to Harrisburg. It took her two days to get there.

Lieutenant Knapp cleaned his equipment and turned it in. He was debriefed and Mr. Knapp checked into a hotel in Harrisburg.

He met Maxine at the train station. He was as impatient and eager as a child on Christmas morning.

When he saw her, he knew the war was over.

After thinking she'd lost him, Maxine felt nothing else mattered but loving him and having him there with her. There was no argument that needed winning, there were no foibles that needed correcting. There was only their love and their life together.

They ran to each other on the train platform. He kissed her and held her up and kissed her some more. He cried for over an hour, cried for all that was lost and all that was regained and all that was yet to come. Emotions were not a part of life in the U.S. Army Air Corps. But this was not the U.S. Army Air Corps. This was life, and she was his wife, and the war was truly over.

—not the end but the beginning—

# CHAPTER #8

# A Memorial Letter to the Family of Sgt. Frank DeGeorge

**A memorial letter about Sgt. Frank DeGeorge. Our top gunner and friend, in the 100th Bomb Group (H), 349th Bomb Squadron.**

To: Frank's son and wife:

Your very thoughtful letter came to me about Frank's passing some time ago. I am very grateful to you for remembering me. It is quite difficult for me to realize that I am the last survivor of the 100th Bomb Group, B-17 we named the "Denver Doll." I am more than grateful that Frank and I got to see each other at the 100th Bomb Group Convention in Salt Lake City. It was great.

Please bear with me, and I will try to tell you, Frank's son and his dear wife, a few things I experienced with this very unusual guy known as Sgt. Frank DeGeorge.

The four officers of this crew came together by a rather funny situation. About thirty of us recently commissioned Lieutenant Pilots, Navigators and Bombardiers were all on an old train, heading for an Air Corps Base somewhere in Texas. After a long four to five hour trip, the train stopped at a place with no buildings in site. It looked liked a place out in the middle of the desert.

As all of us got off the train, the conductor told us that the city of Pyote, Texas was on the other side of the tracks. Someone in a GI truck would pick us up soon!

The train pulled away and on the other side of the tracks was almost nothing! We all began to sing the famous song, "You're in the Army now."

So we began to wait, wait, and wait. We got to know each other quite well then. Imagine thirty men all in the same boat, rather the same sandy desert!

The GI truck did arrive and drove all of us to Rattlesnake Bomber Base.

After we had an Army meal, they began to call off our names. We realized the Commanding Officer was forming up bomber crews. One by one we were being formed up. First came the Pilots and Co-Pilots, then the Navigators. So I heard my name called as the Navigator. Next came the Bombardiers. This set the four of us together for the first time. We were beginning to see whom we would be flying with as a bomber crew. We four asked when we would get to meet the balance of our crew.

About an hour later a large group of men came into the meeting room. The Major announced that these men would be the balance of our crew members. They were gunners, radio operators, crew chiefs, tail gunners—a complete crew support.

The first name called off was Sgt. Frank DeGeorge, assigned to the James McGuire crew as crew chief. He looked good to us, and we all welcomed him. After another long hour, we had the rest of the crew of ten assigned to us. We had a short time to shake hands and learn all the nine new names. But now we knew the men whom we would be with for the duration!

After two days of ground classes by experienced ex-combat men, we were taken out to see our new airplane. It was a large four-engine plane known as a B-17 Flying Fortress. We crawled all over this plane, figuring out where each man would find his position. After a few days of classes, lectures and waiting the four officers of the crew began to realize we had a very capable crew chief and top gunner. He was smart, knew his job and got along well with all the men.

It is important for a crew to work together, not worrying too much about rank. Sgt. DeGeorge understood that all the men were important. Each man had a job to know and do his part.

The first practice mission in our big bomber was gunnery practice. We chased a long rope trailing behind a small plane dragging a white target, about the size of a fighter plane. Sgt. DeGeorge shot from the top turret guns, with the best sight system. He hit the rope and the target sailed to the ground. We all knew we had a dead-on shot on the top turret gun!

The next practice mission was a night navigation flight to practice using the stars and the radio stations. Our Sergeant wanted to know what radio stations in Germany we used to navigate by. I walked right into that question and said I did not know. He answered and said "None, Right?" We got along fine after that.

Later that night, flying at 12,000 feet when all the crew were asleep, except the Navigator and the co-pilot, our Sergeant said. "Look down; there is an airport below." I remarked we were right over the place we were looking for. This gave me a good/bad reputation as now the crew believed I knew what I was doing. Little by little, we became a flying, fighting crew on this big bird.

One day all ten of us were walking toward the flight line hangers for a practice and training mission. Each of us carried a big load of equipment; bags, a parachute, heavy clothing, etc. A ground pounder (non-flying captain) spotted us and required us to stop and listen to his lecture. He insisted that we must all march in step by the book! We officers did not know how to handle this kind of bias and kept quiet. After a few minutes of this dumb talk, our Sergeant asked if he could ask a question. He told the Captain that we were not proud of the way we looked, but we had so much equipment it was difficult to march that way. Could we please go and meet our schedule on the flight line? The Captain was so surprised he ordered us to get going. Our crew knew we had a great crew chief now as he had won the respect of all.

We had been training for a few weeks now and were almost ready to have a week's leave at home before flying overseas. The Navigator was called to report to the Captain at once. Why, no one knows. He informed me to get off this crew and report to a B24 base the next day.

Guess what, I was madder than a wet hen. Here we were working together and were a good team. What happened? Well, I reported to the Base Commander Major with this story. He was furious at the decision of the Captain. The orders were changed and I stayed on with my crew. The Sergeant and I wondered what was at the bottom of this dumb idea.

Later that week, all of us took off and arrived on the Air Corps Base in Grand Island, Nebraska—on time and ready to be on our way overseas. Each had gone home on leave and spent time with wives, family, and friends. But we were not told where we were assigned. We took bets on where we were going. DeGeorge won of course, because he said, "They don't give heavy clothing to GIs on the way to the south Pacific." He was right again.

So, here we are, up in the sky, heading to Goose Bay, way up in northeast Canada. This is the jumping-off point toward combat in England and the European Theatre of Operation (ETO). Some theatre! There were a lot of planes in the air that day. When we landed, the snow was so deep it was piled up higher than the plane on each side of the runway.

One day's rest, one day's lectures, and we took off into the 'wild blue yonder' for merry old England. We flew about twelve hours over the North Atlantic Ocean.

About half way across, as I was navigating by the stars, we ran into heavy clouds. They obscured the stars so much I asked our pilot to climb from 12,000 ft up to 25,000 ft. This let me see all the stars and I could calculate our position and stay on course for England. But one big problem presented itself. We all must get on oxygen, and no more sleeping.

I asked Sgt. DeGeorge to check on everybody every fifteen minutes to make sure they were on oxygen, alive and conscious. He did a super job; he even checked on me. That meant every fifteen minutes he called the roll of all ten men to make sure they answered and were okay. It was cold: 60 degrees below zero! Our heated suits sometimes kept us too warm and might have lulled us to sleep. We were concerned about the men in the ball turret and the tail gunner positions. They were alone; we could not see them. The roll call kept us all awake and in touch.

We landed on time and on course. We came right into the center of Donegal Bay in northern Ireland. I still remember the thrill of seeing the green Island in the middle of the winter. We had left northern Canada with six feet of snow and arrived in a springtime climate! I could not resist asking our Sergeant to awaken all and have them look down at the green.

We landed at the English airdrome, in northern Ireland and had our first culture shock. They ushered us into the dining hall and served all with a large cup of strong English tea, for no coffee was here. I will never forget Sgt. DeGeorge's remark. "Hey, guys, they put a bunch of sugar in the tea." It tasted good and after our long ride in the high sky, it was just what we needed.

After a good night's rest, they sent all ten of us to gunnery school. We learned plenty. The teachers were ex-gunners that had completed twenty-five to thirty missions. Many of them had citations for shooting down enemy fighters. Their teaching was well received.

Next after a boat trip across the sea between Ireland and England, we were riding on a train to the Army Air Corps base near Thorpe Abbotts, in East Anglica, England. It was the famous 100$^{th}$ Heavy Bomb Group. The commanding officer did not take long getting us up on our first practice mission. We needed to learn tight formation flying, and I needed to learn how to guide the big bird into a rendezvous with 12 other B-17s.

Two days later we were on our first combat mission. The Sergeant told us it was to be a milk run. The other flyers had told him this. We did not believe this kind of rumor but it turned out to be true. The reason was easy to figure out; we had fighter cover all the way, and the target was on the French coast. Easy does it. We were no longer rookies.

A few missions later, at about 4:00 a.m. in the morning, I was pulled from that day's mission. Our Bombardier was to do the Navigation job. No reason was given. I never found out why.

But I quickly got all the flight mission navigation data and maps, recorded it for our Bombardier. I was not happy to be without my crew. We were a team and felt safer together. It was a short mission, bombing on the north coast of Normandy where the Germans had anti-aircraft guns and secret weapons.

I waited at the end of the runway for the my crew to return. They were about an hour late. One of the Squadron jeep drivers came out to get me. He told me that the 100$^{th}$ Group had run into very heavy flak, got shot up bad. My crew's B-17 had taken a direct hit in the left wing, exploded and went down. Bang! I almost fainted. It could not be. What had happened? How many chutes were there? Only three. This was the worst mental trauma I had ever faced; I had become an extra Navigator! Try as I did, I never found out much more about this mission.

The problem with grief is that the Air Corps only says, "Go see the Chaplain," which I did. I never missed the Sunday chapel service after that bad news. He taught me to pray for the crew, which I did.

One of my dilemmas was how to inform my wife that I had been pulled from the mission. I talked to the base telegram officer, but he said I couldn't give out any information on any mission period. My wife, Maxine, was living in Denver, Colorado, with the wife of our pilot, Lieutenant Jim McGuire. I knew she would be notified that her husband was missing in action. So I sent my wife Maxine a telegram that said, "Having a good time. Wish you were here." The telegram came the day after Jim's wife had gotten her telegram about his missing in action. These two women figured it out, that John the Navigator was not on this mission.

About two weeks later I got a letter from my wife that told me they got my message very loud and clear. I wonder what the Army censors thought?

After I completed twenty-five combat missions, the Air Corps brass raised the standard missions to thirty. After completing thirty combat missions, they raised the standard missions again to thirty-five. So I flew thirty-five missions!

After completing my tour of missions, I had the right to go home and be reassigned to some other duty, but still as a navigator. Instead, I volunteered to stay over and joined the 100th Bomb Group Intelligence, known as S-2.

The S-2 Major wanted an experienced combat navigator to be on his staff. They knew I was an Architect-Engineer and needed someone who was familiar with reading maps and photos. So, I became a bomb strike, photo-interpreter, and in addition, did the briefing of gunners before they went on missions. I stayed on the ground in England for the balance of the war!

One of the reasons I accepted this assignment was that it gave me access to all the secret information about all of the 100th Group's missions. In my spare time I hunted for the real story of what had happened to my crew on that fateful day. Believe it or not, there was very little information to be found in the files.

For many years after the war was over, I tried to find out where the survivors of my crew were. I knew that the Co-Pilot, the Bombardier, and the Top gunner had bailed out. All the others were killed, but I did not find out about any of the three for ten years until a letter came from our Bombardier John Jones who was living in the south. Never did I find our co-pilot Bradley. I just knew he was somewhere in Texas.

My wife and I stopped and called on Bombardier John Jones on our way to Florida one winter. We spent time visiting at dinner and then went on our way. Talk was brief and not much came out because he did not want to talk about the fateful mission. I understood and did not press him for any story.

You must know how pleased I was when I finally found Frank DeGeorge. All these years with no talk, and then out of the clear blue sky before Christmas came the much-welcomed letter. I called him immediately. It was a joy to me to hear that clear strong voice over the phone again. One of my better Christmas presents.

We arranged to go to the 100th Bomb Group Convention in Salt Lake City together and we saw each other again. It was a wonderful reunion and we had a great time.

This is a big country and to maintain contact is quite difficult when so many people live in different states. I thank you again for keeping me in the loop. I have not retired and still do market research for several of my clients. I live alone as a widower, but have many friends, and many grandchildren—even great grandchildren. Life is interesting and fun, but I still do not know much about what happened to my crew on that fateful day over France!

With kindest regards,
E. John Knapp
1st Lt. Navigator
100th Bomb Group, 349th Squadron

# APPENDIX

## E. John Knapp Biography:

E. JOHN LIVED HIS CHILDHOOD IN BELDING, MICHIGAN, a small town of 2,500 people in the center of Michigan. Belding was a combination of a mill town and agriculture center for the Ionia County area. John's dad operated a barn and house paint factory. John liked working there with his Dad. He remembers making hundreds of gallons of paint and sending it by the railroad to many places in the U.S.

John's education after graduating from Belding High School, was attending Lawrence Tech University, in Southfield, Michigan. He holds degrees in Architecture and Engineering. John studied several graduate courses at the University of Wisconsin in development city planning and related studies.

John was active in the military, having spent nearly four years during WWII, about three years in the UK. He was a 1st Lieutenant Navigator in the 8th Air Corps, 100th Bomb Group. He flew 35 missions in a B-17 heavy bomber against the Nazi war machine. John holds a DFC, an Air Medal with 4 oak clusters, a Victory ETO medal, and a Group Unit Citation.

John and his family moved to Grand Rapids, Michigan in 1952 where he was a principal in the architectural firm of O'Brian & Knapp Associate Architects. The firm designed schools, churches, offices, and homes.

John and his family moved to Madison, Wisconsin in 1966 to establish a branch office for the firm of Daverman Associates, specialists on college campus planning. Five University of Wisconsin master plans were completed.

In 1970 John established the firm of "E. John Knapp, A.I.A., Architect-Analyst" in Madison, Wisconsin. He made a decision to be a specialist in Animal Facility Planning and Design. In 1996 John added Mark Schmidt to the firm, "Knapp Schmidt Architects." This firm has designed over 500 animal care facilities on thirty-six states and four overseas countries.

John published the book, "The Floor Plan Book," containing 100 floor plans of animal facilities for veterinarian hospitals, humane animal shelters and boarding kennels. This book is published by Veterinary Economics Magazine.

In 1998 John became an Architectural Consultant. He moved to St. Paul, Minnesota. He is also an artist, poet and sculptor having exhibited his work in many art galleries in Michigan, Wisconsin, Missouri and Minnesota. He currently lives in Jefferson City, Missouri near his daughter, Marcia.

**Robert Hayes Knapp.** My youngest brother volunteered to serve in the US Navy. The Merchant Marines needed many men. Bob was trained as a signalman, learning all the various signal systems between ships. He was skilled in signal flags, Morse code, and blinking light signals from ship to ship. He served on merchant ships in the Pacific Ocean area. I heard few stories from Bob about his experiences. Like most WWII vets, he didn't like talking about the war.

**Bruce Clifford Knapp.** My younger brother, Bruce, volunteered to serve in the US Navy. The Navy assigned Bruce as a photographer in the submarine corps. His service took him into the Pacific Ocean area. He told stories about picking up downed Air Corps fliers near the Japanese coast. The sub had a lot of other important ventures that he still won't talk about.

Our Mom prayed for us every day. Although all three of us were in combat zones like thousands of others, we were never wounded. I credit Mom and our heavenly Father for our protection. We all returned home to post-War American life with our wives and children.

**Some of the awards E. John Knapp holds:**

Completed 35 combat aerial missions

A Distinguished Flying Cross

An Air Medal with four oak clusters

A Unit Citation

A Victory Europe Metal

Memories of the 349th bomb squadron

—And he lived to tell the tale

## Glossary

| | |
|---|---|
| AC | Army Air Corps |
| AF | Air Force |
| B-17 | B-17 Flying Fortress, 4-Engine Heavy Bomber |
| BG | Bomb Group |
| BG-H | Bomb Group Heavy |
| BIG "B" | Berlin, Germany |
| Buzz bomb | German flying bomb, pilot less |
| Cadet | Beginner in Army officer training schools |
| D-Day | Code word for invasion of Europe |
| EP | English Episcopal Church |
| ETO | European Theater of Operations |
| GIs | Enlisted men, or Government Issue |
| Lt. | Lieutenant |
| M & J | Maxine and John |
| Max | Maxine, John's wife |
| Mess Hall | Dining room |
| Milk run | Combat mission with no opposition |
| Mission | Today's bomber flight in enemy-occupied areas |
| Mom | Maxine Knapp |
| POW | Prisoner of War |
| S-2 | Army Air Intelligence Service |
| SOP | Standard Operating Procedure |
| Strike | Bomb strike-ground target location |
| Vets | Veterans of war |
| WWII | World War Two |

Get Published, Inc!
Thorofare, NJ 08086
09 March, 2010
BA2010068